Interviewing Success

THE INTERVIEWER & INTERVIEWEE...
What You Need to Know

stacey m. macchi & cynthia a. ridle

Western Illinois University

Kendall Hunt
publishing company

Cover images © 2013. Used under license from Shutterstock, Inc.

publishing company

www.kendallhunt.com
Send all inquiries to:
4050 Westmark Drive
Dubuque, IA   52004-1840

Printed in the United States of America
10   9   8   7   6   5   4   3

Contents

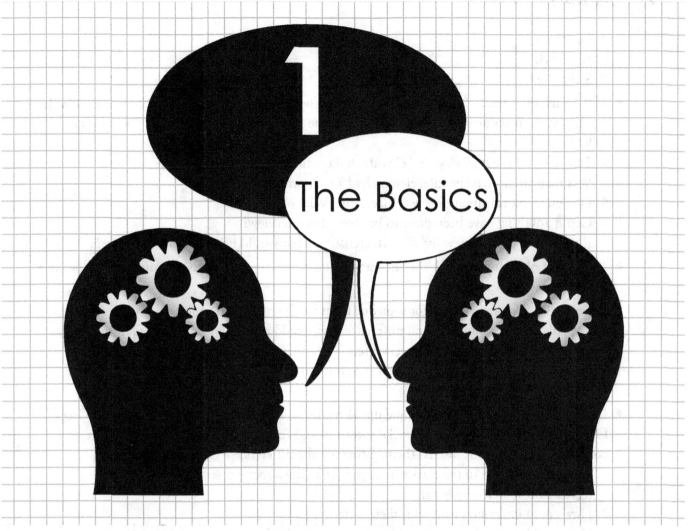

1

The Basics

Image © Danio, 2012. Used under license from Shutterstock, Inc.

e x e r c i s e s

- ◆ Provide a weblink (to an article or another website) that will aid your classmates in the art of interviewing. Provide a brief description of this weblink.
- ◆ Create a list of interviews you have been part of during the last month. Would you characterize these as interviews or social interactions? Why?
- ◆ Interview Log
  - ◇ During the first week (or two) of class, keep a log/list of all interviews that you engage in.
  - ◇ After the week (or two) is over, write a reflection paper about your perceptions of how many interviews you thought you would engage in and how many you actually did engage in.
    - • Does this impact how you see interviews and the role they have in your life?
- ◆ Find a transcript of an interview in written form (newspaper, magazine or book). Try to identify the following items:
  - ◇ Goals of the interview
  - ◇ Who the parties are and what his/her/their purpose may be
  - ◇ Norms

◇ Obstacles
◇ Approach
◇ Structure

- Make a list of characteristics you think exist in "good" interviews. Next, watch an interview. It can be from a news program (e.g., 20/20, Dateline NBC or the Today Show). Then do the following:
  ◇ Talk about if the interview "met" your characteristics. Why or why not?
  ◇ Was it apparent that the interviewers had a relationship? Explain.
  ◇ Do you think this interview was successful? Why or why not?
  ◇ Could anything have been done to improve this interview?
  ◇ If you could create a new list of characteristics, what would be on this list and why?

- Make a list of what you think the advantages and disadvantages are for face to face, online, and telephone interviews.

- Have an international student (or someone from the International Office) visit class. Have this visitor talk about possible cultural differences that could exist in interviews (i.e., norms, dress, nonverbal behaviors, language choices, etc.).
  ◇ Type a reflection paper about how this new cultural information could be used in future interviews.

- Get into groups of four to five. Come up with a list of common stereotypes of those in Greek Organizations (perhaps focus on social sororities and fraternities). After all the groups have come up with their lists, discuss them. What are the differences? Commonalities?
  ◇ Next, ask someone in the class who is part of a Greek social organization why he/she/they feel like those stereotypes exist.
  ◇ How could interviews help with these stereotypes?
  ◇ How could perceptions/stereotypes affect an interview?

- What is a social conversation? What is an interview?
  ◇ The first week of class, engage in dialogue with the other students in the class (five or ten minute conversations) about their lives, coursework, extracurricular activities, etc. The goal is to learn as much as you can in these short conversations.
  ◇ Write a response about the following items:
    • Was this a social interaction or an interview? Why?
    • Did you talk most of the time? Listen most of the time?

d i s c u s s i o n   q u e s t i o n s

- After reading the introductory chapter on interviewing, has your perception of what an interview is changed? If so, describe.

- Did you have any stereotypes of interviews?

- How are interviews different than conversations?

- What do you think is the most prevalent type of interview today? Why?

- What role does self-disclosure have in an interviewing situation?

♦ How important are nonverbal behaviors in interviews?

♦ Describe one interviewing experience you have had and relate the importance of establishing relationships within this interview.

♦ How important do you feel electronic interviews are? Discuss one positive feature of them as well as one negative feature.

♦ In the future, how do you think interviews will continue to change?

♦ Think of an interview you have witnessed or participated in. What made that interview good or what made it bad?

♦ What role do cultural norms have in interviews?

♦ How do stereotypes affect interviews?

♦ How do interviews differ between cultures?

♦ Are there gender differences in interviews?

♦ How do you know?

♦ What are the differences?

Are Today's Grads Unprofessional?

Today's college graduates do not exhibit as much professionalism as their employers expect of them, according to a new study from York College of Pennsylvania.

As part of the small liberal arts college's effort to rebrand itself as a place where "professionalism" is cultivated, its newly created Center for Professional Excellence commissioned a survey of more than 500 human resources professionals and business leaders to gauge not only what they think "professionalism" means but also how well the recent college graduates they have hired exhibit it.

The results of the survey, released Friday, suggest that colleges need to change how they prepare their students for the working world, particularly by reinforcing soft skills like honoring workplace etiquette and having a positive demeanor.

The survey indicates that "there is a widely held sentiment that not all college graduates are displaying professionalism upon entering the work force." More than 37 percent of the respondents reported that "less than half of [the recent graduates they have hired] exhibit professionalism in their first year." The average employer indicated that slightly more than 51 percent of his or her recent hires exhibit "professionalism."

In clarifying what exactly this means, about 88 percent of the respondents "think of professionalism as being related to a person rather than the position." To that end, the traits or behaviors mentioned most by the respondents as being characteristic of professional employees were "personal interaction skills, including courtesy and respect"; "the ability to communicate, which includes listening skills"; "a work ethic which includes being motivated and working on a task until it is complete"; and "appearance."

Similarly, the traits or behaviors most associated by the respondents with "unprofessionalism" included "appearance, which includes attire, tattoos, and piercings"; "poor communication skills including poor grammar"; "poor work ethic"; and "poor attitude."

To further define the gap between employer expectations and student realities, the study asked respondents "to rate traits according to both their importance when considering a person for a position requiring professionalism and the extent to which they are present in first year college educated employees." Upon analysis of these on a matrix, the study notes that the quality most prevalent in new college graduates—"concern about opportunities for advancement"—matters the least to employers.

Among the traits or behaviors employers value most, and that they believe are most deficient in the recent graduates they have hired, include "accepts personal responsibility for decision and actions," "is able to act independently," and "has a clear sense of direction and purpose." The study notes that colleges need to put a particular focus on imparting these traits to their students.

Still, there is some indication that not everyone surveyed believes the "professionalism" of their recent graduate hires has significantly declined in recent years. More than 53 percent of the respondents reported the percentage of those exhibiting "professionalism" has remained the same over the past five years. Nearly a third, however, indicate that it has taken a nosedive in recent years. The most popular reasons for this grim outlook include "an increased sense of entitlement," "new cultural values," and "a changed work ethic."

David Polk, the professor of behavioral science at York whose research group conducted this survey, said he was unsure how much the responses indicated some sort of "generational phenomenon," acknowledging the age-old disappointment adults throughout history have often expressed in the younger generation. He noted with disappointment that the survey failed to ask the ages of those responding. Still, he noted that, generally, those responding were significantly older than the recent graduates they were asked to assess.

"One of the things you've got to ask yourself is, are we just a bunch of dinosaurs looking at young people saying, 'What I'm seeing here is inappropriate,' " mused Polk, who made sure to note he was 61. "Are the changes in attitude here generational or are they lifestyle changes? Will you people eventually take on conservative professionalism or have things just changed? We'll have to do more studies to find out. For instance, the freewheeling baby boomers of the 1960s are the ones who filled out our survey today. We can be sure which it is with just this one study."

Polk's students, who have been discussing his research findings in class, are of two minds about what employers are saying about their generation. On one hand, Polk said he has students balk at the notion that certain tattoos or piercings might make them seem "unprofessional." Conversely, he said nearly all of them admit to having a greater sense of "entitlement." While Polk said that most students did not think of this as being problematic, he expressed some concern in this attitude.

"We tell our children, 'You're all worth something,' and 'None of you are losers,' " Polk said. "I've asked my class, 'Do you really think you're all winners in everything?' I mean, you've got to be mediocre in something. This attitude that everyone's going to play on the team and that everyone is going to be recognized for something is out there. It's great that people have positive self-esteem, but I can't help but think that we live in Lake Wobegon [the fictional town of *A Prairie Home Companion* fame], where every student is 'above average.' "

Despite this, Polk offered a number of suggestions about what colleges can do in the classroom to improve the "professionalism" of their graduates.

"I think if you can get professors to buy into the concept, which is critical, then professors can serve as role models," Polk said. "For instance, the last thing I would do is wear blue jeans to class. I think that's unprofessional and not something I'd wear in a position of presumed authority. . . . Also, some professors will say, 'Just call me by my first name.' There's no way I think that's proper behavior in my classroom. It creates this wonderfully false impression that professors are less authority figures than they are friends."

Professors can lead by example in other ways, too, Polk continued.

"Let's just ignore parents for a second, and let's call students out on improper behavior in the classroom," Polk said. "You'll probably notice from the study, a lot of what people are talking about here is soft skills like attitude, demeanor and respect. As a professor, most of us see our jobs as conveying knowledge and making sure our students comprehend it. I'm not sure how many would respond that it is also their job to help a student develop good behavior. There's this moral authority that some professors get uncomfortable with. For this to work successfully, when a professor calls out a student's behavior, the administration should be there to back them up immediately and say, 'Your behavior is wrong.' "

In the meantime, York's Center for Professional Excellence has gotten in on the act. It will host a number of seminars throughout the academic year with employers talking about expectations of their employees and other workplace issues. Polk said he would like students to be required to attend a certain number of these seminars throughout their college careers. Additionally, he noted he could see the potential for York to create something akin to a general education course focusing on "professionalism."

"If we can truly embrace this thing, it'll be a major challenge," said Polk of York's effort to rebrand itself. "I can just see me going to faculty and saying to them, 'Your blue jeans are inappropriate,' and them telling me where I can go."

—David Moltz

Are Today's Grads Unprofessional?

A recent survey conducted by York College of Pennsylvania on professionalism revealed some behaviors, characteristics, and traits that employers see in recent college graduates. See how close your answers to the following questions match the respondents (employers of recent graduates) answers.

1. How do you think professionalism of today's college graduates compares with the professionalism exhibited by graduates five years ago?

   a. Today's college graduates exhibit MORE professionalism
   b. Today's college graduates exhibit LESS professionalism
   c. There has been no change in professionalism

2. Which of the following behaviors do you believe employers mentioned most as being characteristic of professionalism from employees?

   _____courtesy and respect   _____ability to communicate   _____listening skills

   _____motivation   _____physical appearance   _____grammar

   _____staying on task until completion   _____attitude

3. Which of the following traits or behaviors do you believe employers value most in new college graduate employees?

   _____clear sense of direction and purpose   _____concerned about advancement
                                                   opportunities

   _____accepts personal responsibility for   _____acts independently
   decision and actions

4. Employers who have seen a decline in professionalism believe the reasons for the decline are: an increased sense of entitlement, new cultural values, and a changed work ethic.

Do you believe these could be the reasons for the decline? _____

_____   _____

What other reasons do you believe could attribute to the decline? _____

_____

_____

Note Taking Interview Practice

As an interviewer it is important that you be able to take notes as well as maintain sufficient eye contact and follow a list of questions. Most beginning interviewers find this very difficult. Most students reveal that one of their biggest problems while conducting interviews is note taking.

This assignment will help you:

1. Practice interviewing skills including listening and questioning skills.
2. Practice effective note taking while maintaining eye contact.

Choose a classmate for this interviewing practice. You will each participate in a 10 minute interview.

As an interviewer it is your goal to elicit as much information as you possibly can from the interviewee about one of the following topics:

1. An interesting, unusual or exciting/memorable event about the interviewee.
2. A pet peeve or frustrating/disappointing event in the life of the interviewee.

Instructions for Interviewer

Before beginning your interview, decide on one of the above topics. Create several questions, including follow-up questions for your interviewee.

During the interview, do not write complete answers to every question. Use key words only. Try to maintain sufficient eye contact with your interviewee.

Instructions for Interviewee

As an interviewee you must listen closely and answer the questions accurately. If the interviewer asks a closed question then answer with just a one or two word answer. Do not provide more information than is requested.

Upon completion of both interviews take turns completing this final step in the interview. Using your notes, summarize to the interviewee the information you received to make sure you have the correct information and understand what was provided during the interview.

Take a few minutes to reflect on your note taking and eye contact throughout the interview process. What goals would you like to set for yourself in regards to maintaining eye contact and taking effective notes? How do you plan to reach these goals?

Interview Critique

Objective/Directions: For this assignment, you will need to critique two interviews. A critique (for our course) will be an essay that analyzes a presentation or other performance event according to criteria that are accepted as standard in the field. The two interviews that you watch need to be on the web or on the television and be at least 10 minutes long (each). Some suggestions would include: Barbara Walters, Oprah, Larry King, Piers Morgan, Dr. Phil, etc.

Assignment: After watching the interviews you will write your interview critique essay. Remember, you must apply your knowledge of interviewing elements in evaluating an interview outside of class. The essay should be two to three pages long, double spaced and reveal how well each interview met the criteria of an effective interview based on what you have learned about interviewing in class to date. Make sure to include the following components and answer the following questions.

- An introductory paragraph
  - This paragraph needs to explain the event, noting the names of the parties involved, the title of the interview, show, audience, and purpose for the interview.
- How did the relationship between the parties affect the interview?
- How did the gender of the parties affect the interview (disclosure, nonverbal, etc.)?
- Which party controlled the interview?
  - Why do you believe this person had control and/or direction?
- What was the level (or amount) of self-disclosure, risk and type of content exchanged?
- What verbal and nonverbal interactions affected the interview situation and how?
- How did situational and environmental variables influence the interview?
- How do you think family, associations, government agencies, and professional associations of the parties involved influenced the outcome of the interview?
- What type of questions did the interviewer use?
  - How could the questions have been improved?
- Were the opening and closing sufficient? Explain.
  - How could they be improved?
- What could each party have done differently to improve the interview?

Name _____ Date _____

Here I Am!

This personal fact sheet will help your instructor get to know you better as you begin this course. This information sheet will only be seen by the instructor and serves a few purposes.

Purpose (1): By gaining an understanding of who you are, your instructor can work to adapt this course to best serve the needs of those in it.

Purpose (2): By gaining an understanding of your experiences, your instructor can work to ensure that your interview partner has similar yet complementary differences.

Name: _____

Campus Address: _____

Phone Number: _____ Email: _____

Class Standing: Freshman   Sophomore   Junior   Senior

Expected Graduation Date: _____

Hometown: _____

High School: _____ Public   Private

Technical/Vocational/Specialized School:

_____

Other colleges/universities attended:

_____

If you earned a degree from another college/university, please specify: _____

_____

Military Background: _____

Major: _____ Minor: _____

Internship Experience: _____

_____

Have you taken courses that are related to Interviewing?   Yes   No

If yes, please list below:

Course Name	When	What Institution (college/university, etc.)
_____	_____	_____
_____	_____	_____
_____	_____	_____
_____	_____	_____

Why are you taking this course? _____

_____

_____

What do you hope to learn by the end of this course? _____

_____

_____

Have you had any interviewing experiences?   Yes   No

If yes, please list: _____

What is your desired profession (upon graduation)? _____

  Why? _____

Are you currently (or soon to be) involved in searches for a job (part- or full-time) or internship?

Yes   No

  If yes, please describe: _____

_____

Basics of Interviewing

An interview is a communication process and there is a sharing between the two parties involved. Each party may influence the other party and the parties share simultaneously. Interviewing does share some common characteristics with social conversations, small groups, and public speaking presentations, but they are also very different. In the chart below explain in your own words how each communication situation is different and similar from an interview situation. The first one is completed as an example.

	Public Speech	Small Group	Social Conversation	Interview
Parties Involved	There is a speaker and an audience. The audience may be passive in a public speech and in an interview the parties must both be active participants. The speaker is expected to talk the majority of the time except for the question and answer part of a speech, while during an interview both parties are expected to contribute to the interview throughout the interview.	In some small groups there are assigned roles (parties) but in many there are no roles and the group is expected to work together as a team to complete their task/objective. In an interview, each person has a role or a part and must cooperate in order to have a successful interview.	During a social conversation anyone can join and ask and share information at any time. The topic may shift several times and rapidly during the conversation and there is no role for each individual participating in a social conversation.	In an interview there is an interviewee party and an interviewer party. Each party may consist of more than one person and each party must come prepared to the interview in order for it to be successful.
Goal/Objective				

continued

	Public Speech	Small Group	Social Conversation	Interview
Structure				
Verbal Communication				

Types of Interviews

There are numerous types of interviews and although the types do overlap, the objective of the interview will help define the type. Four of the most common types of interviews are:

Information gathering interview

Selection interview

Persuasive interview

Helping interview

Listed below are several scenarios. Match the scenario to the correct type of interview.

1. Jamie is interested in a career in pharmaceutical sales. In order to learn more about this career Jamie will interview an individual who has been a pharmaceutical sales representative for ten years. Her goal is to learn as much as she can about this type of career. Jamie is conducting a(n)

   _____.

2. Amber is a physician's assistant at the recently opened medical clinic. Her area of specialty is geriatrics. Amber must interview each new patient and determine their health history, status, and needs. Amber is conducting a(n)

   _____.

3. José is a counselor at the University Counseling Center. His day is filled with interviewing and counseling students who have addiction tendencies. José is engaged in a(n)

   _____.

4. Aerial Manufacturing Company has just opened a new plant in Chicago, Illinois. The Director of Human Resources will be conducting interviews over the next three weeks to determine which applicants are the best fit for the director and manager positions at the plant. The Director of Human Resources is conducting a(n)

   _____.

5. Chris is a car salesman and is trying to close the sale of a new pickup truck to Lester. Chris is conducting a(n)

_____.

6. Robert is a reporter for the student-run television station on campus. He has just arrived on the scene of a fire in one of the residence halls. Robert is interviewing a police officer and a fireman on the scene in order to get as much information about the incident for his story. Robert is conducting a(n)

_____.

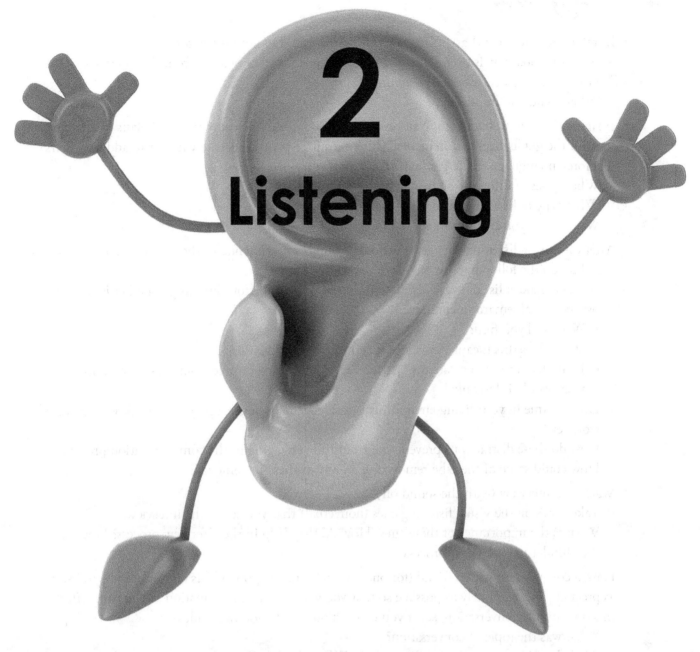

2
Listening

Image © Julien Tromeur, 2012. Used under license from Shutterstock, Inc.

e x e r c i s e s

♦ (In Class): Select a partner. Have a conversation with your partner about your future career goals, the most exciting moment in your life thus far, the reason you wanted to take this interviewing class, etc. or any topic you like. After each of you is done, you will be asked to "introduce" your partner to the rest of the class but notes cannot be used!

♦ (In Class): Select a partner. Have a conversation with your partner about (your future career goals, the most exciting moment in your life thus far, the reason you wanted to take this interviewing class, etc.) or any topic you like. When you are engaged in this activity, note what types of techniques you used (and the other person used) when listening. Also make note if mirroring/paraphrasing was used (and how it helped or hindered the conversation).

- Listen to an interview (Larry King, Piers Morgan, etc). Do not take notes.
  - ◇ After the interview is over, write down anything you can remember from the interview.
  - ◇ How would you classify your listening skills?
  - ◇ What could you improve?

- Imagine that you were chosen to sit on a committee at the university that had plans to change some of the graduation requirements? This committee plans to debate whether to add two years of a foreign language to the graduation requirement.
  - ◇ What types of information would you listen for?
  - ◇ What type of listening would you use?
  - ◇ Who would you be most interested to listen to?

- After discussing listening engage in various "setting" experiments. In the various "settings" of your life, do the following (for one day):
  - ◇ In class, make a list of every distraction that prevents you from listening (whether it is psychological, environmental, etc.).
    - • What did you find?
    - • What does this mean? How does this impede your learning?
    - • If you had to try to create the "perfect" class environment, free from these distractions, what would it look like?
  - ◇ Do the same in your living environment (residence hall, house, apartment, etc.), your place of work, etc.
  - ◇ How do these distractions prevent you from fully engaging in the communication process?
  - ◇ How could some of these be removed? Can any of these be removed?

- Watch an interview (with the sound off).
  - ◇ Take notes on the visual listening cues (nonverbal) that you see in the interview.
  - ◇ What is the importance of these cues? How do they help in the interview process? How do they hinder the interview process?

- Have a conversation with a friend (for one minute). The purpose of this conversation is to listen as precisely and accurately as possible so that you gain as much information as you can. After this one minute conversation, see if you can respond to the following ideas:
  - ◇ What was the topic of conversation?
  - ◇ Were there barriers to your ability to listen? If so, describe?
  - ◇ Do you feel you listened closer knowing you were going to have to report on your conversation? Why or why not?
  - ◇ What did you learn about effectively listening?

- Make a list of characteristics that you think good listeners have.
  - ◇ Watch an interview (from any media source).
  - ◇ Compare your list of characteristics to the interviewer/interviewee.
  - ◇ How do you plan to develop your skills?

d i s c u s s i o n   q u e s t i o n s

- Are there barriers to listening during an interview? If so, describe.
- In an interview, do you feel there is a difference between listening and hearing? If so, describe.
- What type of listening do you think you engage in the most? Why?
- If you were to give suggestions of how you could become a better listener, what would you say?
- What type(s) of barriers do we face when it comes to listening?
- How does mirroring relate to listening?
- How is paraphrasing related to listening?
- How are listening and perception related?
- How do we listen visually? Aurally? Culturally?
- Does language affect our ability to listen? If yes, how?
- How does listening differ depending on the type of interview we are engaged in?
- One of the most important skills in the business world is listening.
  - ◇ Do you think this is true? Why? Who in the business world listens? For what reasons?
  - ◇ What are the implications for not listening effectively in the business world?
- Think about an interview that you were part of. What type of listening did you engage in?
  - ◇ How do you know?

Name _____ Date _____

Your Hurier Listening Profile

Complete the listening questionnaire on the following pages. Each question corresponds with one of the six listening components you've learned about: Hearing, Understanding, Remembering, Interpreting, Evaluating and Responding.

It might be fun, before you go any further, to guess how you will do.

I think I will score highest on the component of _____~~IS~~_____.

I will probably score lowest on the component of _____~~I~~_____.

Now, respond to each of the following questions concerning *your perception* of your listening behavior. Write the appropriate number in the blank to your left, using the following key. Unless your instructor gives you other directions, *choose one specific listening context* and answer all questions with that situation in mind. This will help you be more consistent in your responses.

Key:

5 = almost always

4 = usually

3 = sometimes

2 = infrequently

1 = almost never

__5__ 1. I am constantly aware that people and circumstances change over time.

__5__ 2. I take into account the speaker's personal and cultural perspective when listening to him.

__5__ 3. I pay attention to the most important things going on around me.

__4__ 4. I accurately hear what is said to me.

__4__ 5. I understand my partner's vocabulary and recognize that my understanding of a word is likely to be somewhat different from the speaker's.

__4__ 6. I adapt my response according to the needs of the particular situation.

_4_ 7. I easily follow conversations and can accurately recall which member contributed which ideas in small-group discussions.

_5_ 8. I consider my partner's personal expertise on the subject when she tries to convince me to do something.

_4_ 9. I do not let my emotions interfere with my listening or decision making.

_4_ 10. I can remember what the instructor has said in class even when it's not in the book.

_4_ 11. I recognize my "hot buttons," and don't let them influence my listening.

_4_ 12. I take into account the person's motives, expectations, and needs when determining the meaning of the message.

_4_ 13. I provide clear and direct feedback to others.

_5_ 14. I let the speaker know immediately that he has been understood.

_4_ 15. I overcome distractions such as the conversation of others, background noises, and telephones, when someone is speaking.

_4_ 16. I enter communication situations with a positive attitude.

_5_ 17. I am sensitive to the speaker's tone of voice in communication situations.

_6_ 18. I listen to and accurately remember what my partner says, even when I strongly disagree with his viewpoint.

_6_ 19. I encourage information sharing by creating a climate of trust and support.

_5_ 20. I concentrate on what the speaker is saying, even when the information is complicated.

_5_ 21. I consider how the speaker's facial expressions, body posture, and other nonverbal behaviors relate to the verbal message.

_5_ 22. I weigh all evidence before making a decision.

_5_ 23. I take time to analyze the validity of my partner's reasoning before arriving at my own conclusions.

Your Hurier Listening Profile *continued*

_5_ 24. I am relaxed and focused in important communication situations.

_3_ 25. I listen to the entire message without interrupting.

_4_ 26. I make sure that the physical environment encourages effective listening.

_4_ 27. I recognize and take into account personal and cultural differences in the use of time and space that may influence listening effectiveness.

_5_ 28. I ask relevant questions and restate my perceptions to make sure I have understood the speaker correctly.

_5_ 29. I listen carefully to determine whether the speaker has solid facts and evidence or whether he is relying on emotional appeals.

_4_ 30. I am sensitive to my partner's feelings in communication situations.

_4_ 31. I have a wide variety of interests that helps me approach tasks creatively.

_4_ 32. I distinguish between main ideas and supporting evidence when I listen.

_4_ 33. I am ready to focus my attention when a presenter begins her talk.

_4_ 34. I readily consider new evidence and circumstances that might prompt me to reevaluate my previous position.

_5_ 35. I can recall what I have heard, even when I am in stressful situations.

_4_ 36. I take notes effectively when I believe it will enhance my listening.

After completing all questions, you can figure out your score.

159

80
76
3
___
159

Identifying Your Listening Profile

- ◆ Transfer your self-ratings for each question to the corresponding question numbers. For instance, if you gave yourself a 4 on Question 1, you would find Question 1, under Evaluating, and would put a 4 on the appropriate line. Continue for all 36 questions.
- ◆ Total the points you assigned for each of the six sets of questions.
- ◆ Place your total for each component in the *Total* space.

HEARING	UNDERSTANDING	REMEMBERING
4 _4_	5 _4_	3 _5_
15 _4_	11 _4_	7 _4_
16 _4_	25 _3_	10 _4_
20 _5_	28 _5_	18 _5_
24 _5_	32 _4_	31 _4_
33 _4_	36 _4_	35 _5_
_26_ Total	_24_ Total	_27_ Total

INTERPRETING	EVALUATING	RESPONDING
2 _5_	1 _5_	6 _4_
12 _4_	8 _5_	9 _4_
14 _5_	22 _5_	13 _4_
17 _5_	23 _5_	19 _5_
21 _5_	29 _5_	26 _4_
30 _4_	34 _4_	27 _4_
_28_ Total	_29_ Total	_25_ Total

Let's look at what this information tells you about your self-perceptions regarding your listening behavior. Transfer your totals for each component to the *Total Points* column (which follows). Rank order each of the six components according to your totals.

	Total Points	Rank
COMPONENT I: Hearing	26	
COMPONENT II: Understanding	24	
COMPONENT III: Remembering	27	
COMPONENT IV: Interpreting	28	
COMPONENT V: Evaluating	29	
COMPONENT VI: Responding	25	

Name _____ Date _____

Your Hurier Listening Profile *continued*

Use the following guide to assess each skill area:

25-30 points: you see yourself as an excellent listener

20-25 points: you believe you are a good listener

15-20 points: you consider your listening skills adequate

10-15 points: you perceive some problems in your listening behavior

Now consider:

- In what skill area are you high? *evaluating*
- Which one do you see as a potential problem? *understanding - patience!*
- How did your actual ranking compare with your earlier guess? *higher than guessed.*
- Is there a particular component with a significantly different total—either much higher or much lower than the others? *No*
- How do you think someone else would rank your listening behaviors? Take the role of your roommate, your parents, or some other person who knows you well and answer the questionnaire from that person's perspective. How did you do?

Keep these results in mind as you cover the specific listening skills throughout this text.

REFERENCES

Abbott, J. (2007). Intrapersonal communication and well-being. The University of North Dakota Press. 126 pp. AAT 3277020.

Anderson, D. A. (2000). Effective communicative and listening skills revisited. *Marine Corps Gazette. 84*(3), 60–61.

Bowman, J., & Klopping, L. (1999). Bandstands, bandwidth, and business communication: Technology and the sanctity of writing. *Business Communication Quarterly, 62*(1), 82–90.

Boyle, R. C. (1999). A manager's guide to effective listening. *Manage, 51*(1), 6–7.

Bentley, S. C. (1998). Listening better. *Nursing Homes, 47*(2), 56–60.

Brownell, J. (1994a). Creating strong listening environments: A key hospitality management task. *The International Journal of Contemporary Hospitality Management, 6*(3), 3–10.

Brownell, J. (1994b). Listening and career development in the hospitality industry. *Journal of the International Listening Association, 8*, 31–49.

Brownell, J., & Reynolds, D. (2002). Strengthening the food and beverage purchaser-supplier partnership: Actions that make a difference. *Cornell Hotel & Restaurant Administration Quarterly, 42*(4), 1–13.

Collingwood, H. (2001, December). Leadership's first commandment: Know thyself. *Harvard Business Review,* Special Issue, 8–13.

Conchie, B. (2007, September). Seven demands of leadership. *Leadership Excellence, 24*(9), 18–21.

Cooper, L. O. (1997). Listening competency in the workplace: A model for training. *Business Communication Quarterly, 60*(4), 75–84.

Daly, J. A., Vangelista, A. L., & Daughton, S. M. (1987). *The nature and correlates of conversational sensitivity.* Paper presented at the annual meeting of the Speech Communication Association Convention, Boston, MA.

Elias, M. (September 23, 2003). The doctor is inattentive: Med students will be tested on empathy, listening skills. *USA Today,* p. D9.

Feiertag, H. (2002). Listening skills, enthusiasm top list of salespeople's best traits. *Hotel & Motel Management, 217*(13), 20.

Gesell, I. (2007). Am I talking to me? The power of internal dialogue to help or hinder our full-body listening. *The Journal for Quality and Participation, 30*(3), 22–24.

Goby, J., & Lewis, H. (2000). The key role of listening in business: A study of the Singapore insurance industry. *Business Communication Quarterly, 63*(2), 41–51.

Goleman, D. (1998). *Working with emotional intelligence.* New York: Bantam Books.

Haferkamp, C. J. (1989). Implications of self-monitoring theory for counseling supervision. *Counselor Education and Supervision, 28*(4), 290–298.

Howell, W. S. (1982). *The empathic communicator.* Belmont, CA: Wadsworth Publishers.

Hulnick, E. (2000). Doing business virtually. *Communication World, 17*(3), 33–36.

Johnson, S. D., & Bechler, C. (1998). Examining the relationship between listening effectiveness and leadership emergence: Perceptions, behaviors, and recall. *Small Group Research, 29*(4), 452–471.

Kemp, M. (2000). Listening skill saves time, increases effectiveness. *The American Salesman, 45*(9), 3–8.

Lundsteen, S. (1993). Metacognitive listening. In A.D. Wolvin and C.G. Coakley (Eds.), *Perspectives on Listening,* pp. 106–123. Norwood, NJ: Ablex Publishing.

McMaster, M. (1999). An intrapersonal systems view of communication. *The Union Institute.* 221 p. AAT 9939838.

Miller, A. (1996). Using probing skills to uncover customer needs. *Telemarketing and Call Center Solutions, 15*(5), 72–75.

Neville, M. G. (2008). Using appreciative inquiry and dialogical learning to explore dominant paradigms. *Journal of Management Education, 32*(1), 98–110.

Pedersen-Pietersen, L. (1999). Reworking education in a virtual schoolhouse, *New York Times, Late Edition,* (3), 13.

Peters, T., & Austin, N. (1985). *A passion for excellence.* New York: Warner Books.

Purdy, M. (1991). Intrapersonal and interpersonal listening. In D. Borisoff and M. Purdy (Eds.), *Listening in Everyday Life: A Personal and Professional Approach,* p. 21–58. New York: University Press of America.

Rea, A., Hoger, B., & Rooney, P. (1999). Communication and technology: Building bridges across the chasm. *Business Communication Quarterly, 62*(2), 92–96.

Render, M. (2000). Better listening makes for a better marketing message. *Marketing News, 34*(19), 22.

Your Hurier Listening Profile *continued*

Rhodes, S., Watson, K. W., & Barker, L. L. (1990). Listening assessment: Trends and influencing factors in the 1980s. *Journal of the International Listening Association, 4,* 62–82.

Salopek, J. (1999). Is anyone listening? *Training & Development, 53*(9), 58–59.

Snyder, M. (1974). Self-monitoring of expressive behavior. *Journal of Personality and Social Psychology, 30,* 526–637.

Steil, L. K., & Bommelje, R. K. (2004). *Listening leaders: The 10 golden rules to listen, lead, and succeed.* St. Paul, MN: Beaver's Pond Press.

Tapscott, D., Ticoll, D., & Lowy, A. (2000). *Digital capital: Harnessing the power of business webs.* Boston: Harvard Business School Press.

Walther, J. (1996). Computer-mediated communication: Impersonal, interpersonal, and hyperpersonal interaction. *Communication Research, 23*(1), 3–11.

Welch, D. V. (1998). Reflective leadership: The stories of five leaders successfully building generative organizational culture. *The Union Institute.* 151 p. AAT 9910836.

Wilmot, W. W. (1987). *Perception of the other: Dyadic communication.* New York: McGraw-Hill.

Are You a Good Listener?

Directions: Read the articles "Is Anyone Listening" by Jennifer Salopek, "Six Ways To Be A Better Listener" by Paul Blodgett, "Listening: A Vital Skill" by Kenneth Petress and "Now Hear This: Without Listening, There Is No Communication" by John Ward. Complete the following questions based upon the readings above.

"Is Anyone Listening"
Author: Jennifer Salopek

http://www.accessmylibrary.com/coms2/summary_0286-9334471_ITM

1. What are the explanations given for why people are poor listeners?
2. Do you agree with these explanations? Why or why not?
3. Do you think technology is contributing to our decrease in listening skills? Why or why not?
4. Explain how you will use listening in your personal/professional life.
5. What suggestions do you have to be a better listener?
6. Suggest an activity that you and your classmates can do to help "become" better listeners.
7. Do you agree or disagree that listening needs practice, support, and reward?
8. Which "be a better listener tip" do you identify with the most? Why?

"Six Ways To Be a Better Listener"
Author: Paul C. Blodgett

http://connection.ebscohost.com/c/articles/9708292048/six-ways-be-better-listener

1. What are six ways that you can become a better listener? Do you agree with these? Why or why not?
2. After reading this article what goals would you like to set for becoming a better listener in your personal/professional life?
3. In what ways can you encourage another person to continue speaking?
4. Does the sound of your voice impact your listening abilities? How?
5. What is the best way to let a speaker know that you've heard him/her?
6. How important do you feel reflecting is to the listening process?

"Listening: A Vital Skill"
Author: Kenneth Petress

http://www.thefreelibrary.com/Listening%3a+A+Vital+Skill.-a062980773

1. In your words, define listening.
2. How would faculty, staff, students, and administration benefit from better listening (provide reasons for all the above groups)?
3. How important is listening during an interview?
4. List four characteristics/traits of good listeners.
5. Name the advantages of good listening.
6. Do you pay close attention to others when listening? Explain.

"Now Hear This: Without Listening There Is No Communication"
Author: John R. Ward

http://www.thefreelibrary.com/Now+hear+this%3A+without+listening,+there+is+no+communication.-a08619898

1. What is listening?
2. Who was Chester Carlson and why was listening important to him?
3. If communication is going to "work" what must occur?
4. What are Kipling's six servants? Explain how these function in your life.
5. Why is looking part of listening?
6. What does good listening include?
7. What types of information do you miss due to poor listening? Explain.
8. Do you listen with all your senses? How?
9. What type of attitude should we have when engaged in listening?

Final Question to Consider: How can you improve your listening skills? Give at least three suggestions.

Listening Activity/Response Paper Assignment

This activity and paper assignment is meant to encourage you to apply the listening concepts discussed in class and in your text. We usually participate in communication situations and do not think about listening concepts. This assignment will help you think more critically about your listening skills. For one week, you will record your listening habits. During this time, you should try to make improvements in your listening habits based upon information/suggestions in your text. Record the results of these attempts. At the end of the week, you will be asked to write a response paper about this process.

1. For one week, you will record the types of listening you feel you engage in. This should be completed after conversations with others. Make sure you have at least seven conversations recorded each day. Each entry should include: the date, time, conversation location, context, and the name of the other party. Also include information about this conversation partner such as how you know this person, (friend, family member, co-worker, acquaintance, etc.), age, how long you've known this individual and if this is someone with whom you communicate on a regular basis.

2. At the end of the week, you will write a one page reflection paper about your experiences. In this paper, you should include a discussion of the following:
   ◊ What types of listening you used (according to those listed in your text)? What obstacles to listening (if any) did you experience? Did you do anything to overcome these obstacles? If yes, how? If not, why not?
   ◊ What did you notice about your listening habits? Explain both good and bad.
   ◊ What did you notice about the listening habits of others? Explain both good and bad.
   ◊ After this week, what goals would you like to set to improve your listening habits?

Listening and Recall

You are a student who works at the university newspaper. A major world news story is occurring and you have to write an article about it for the next edition of the paper. Watch and record a newscast or interview from ABC, CBS, NPR, CNN, etc. that is covering this major world news story. View the interview while you are also recording it. Do not take any notes while watching the interview. As soon as the interview is finished write down the answers to the following questions (from memory).

1. List or outline the information from this interview/newscast that you feel is important and should appear in your article.
2. List what nonverbal behaviors and/or verbal language was exhibited by the interview parties that may reveal their mood, emotion, etc.
3. Write/list the questions you would like to ask the interviewee about this topic if you get the opportunity.
4. Write down the quotations that you remember.
5. Write any other information that you remember from the interview.

Now, play the recording again (for a second time) and check the accuracy of your answers.

Reflect on the following:

♦ How well did you listen and recall information?

♦ What do you need to work on to become a better listener?

♦ How can you improve your recall?

Practice this activity over and over again to check your own listening and recall skills.

Listening Research Activity

Individually, or with a partner, choose one of the following listening topics. Conduct research on this topic and come to the next class period prepared to present your portion of the topic during class.

Listening Topics

1. Poor listening skills and why most people are poor listeners.

2. What is the difference between hearing and listening?

3. How does verbal and nonverbal communication affect listening?

4. Types of listening and why it is important to understand each.

5. Do different cultures listen differently?

6. What are the ethical considerations and moral responsibilities of listening?

7. Suggestions on how to change poor listening habits.

8. Guidelines for effective listening.

9. Resources for evaluating and improving listening skills.

Based on the information provided in the presentations, how would you evaluate yourself as a listener?

List three recommendations that you would like to put into practice in your life in order to improve your listening skills. Explain how you can incorporate these into your daily life.

What's My Listening Goal?

It is important to be aware of the different types of listening and to know which type of listening to use in a variety of settings. It is also advantageous to determine which type(s) of listening you are best at and which type(s) you need to work on. Read each scenario below and determine which type(s) of listening would be most effective for the situation.

Choose from the following listening types:

Comprehension/Remembering

Enjoyment/Pleasure

Empathy/Understanding

Resolution/Problem Solving

Evaluation/Critique/Judgment

Scenario 1: Tom has landed his dream job as a district manager with a national chain. He is attending a week-long training session at the corporate headquarters. Which type of listening should Tom use? Why?

_____

_____

_____

_____

Scenario 2: Penny plans to vote in the next election at her school for the Student Government Association president. There are several important decisions that the president will need to make in the next year. There are two candidates who are qualified and very conscientious. Penny is attending a debate between the candidates. Which type of listening should Penny use? Why?

_____

_____

_____

_____

Scenario 3: Bill has had a very stressful day of classes at school. After classes he went to practice for the spring musical and during dinner he had an argument with his significant other. Bill retreats to his room and listens to his favorite music. Which type of listening will Bill use? Why?

_____

_____

_____

_____

Scenario 4: Markio has recently suffered a bad break up with his significant other. Markio wants to meet you, his good friend, for dinner in the dining hall and share with you what happened. Which type of listening should you be prepared to use? Why?

_____

_____

_____

_____

What's My Listening Goal? *continued*

Scenario 5: The sales team at XMJ Corporation has experienced high turnover the last three years and this turnover has affected sales and the commissions for the sales staff. The Director of Sales has called a meeting with all of the sales staff to discuss the cause for the turnover and to gather ideas to remedy the turnover. Which type of listening will the sales team use? Why?

_____

_____

_____

_____

What are the consequences for using the wrong type of listening in some situations (for example, using critical listening when you should use relationship listening)?

_____

_____

_____

_____

3
Questions

Image © froxx, 2012. Used under license from Shutterstock, Inc.

e x e r c i s e s

♦ If you could interview a famous person, who would it be? Why? Write ten questions that you would ask this person. Additionally, please identify each question in three ways: neutral/leading/threatening, open/closed, and primary/secondary.

♦ Get a copy of a local or national newspaper and find one article that you find interesting. Imagine that you were going to interview the author of that article. Write 10 primary questions you would ask and 10 secondary/probing questions.

♦ Imagine that you could interview any professor you had. What would you want to ask him/her? Write 10 questions. Now, go over your list again. Identify each as neutral/leading/threatening, open/closed, and primary/secondary.

♦ Make a list of ten occupations where you think questions are extremely relevant. What skills do these individuals need to have for these occupations? How important are questions to these individuals? What if their questions have problems? How would it affect the job of this individual? Choose one of these occupations and go talk to someone who has a career in this occupation. Ask how important questions are to their daily job/routine.

- Identify the problems in the following questions. Rephrase each question to make it a good question. Avoid problems in your revised question. Don't change the original question.
  ◇ Tell me about the tornado? Was it scary?
  ◇ You are going to vote in the election, aren't you?
  ◇ (Asked by a doctor) Did your knee start giving you trouble after the basketball game?
  ◇ How are the lectures and the readings in this course?
  ◇ Do you like this university because of the choice in majors?

- Watch any Larry King/Oprah/Barbara Walters/Piers Morgan interview. Identify the following after watching this interview:
  ◇ Number of open questions vs. number of closed questions.
    • Why is this relevant/significant?
  ◇ How would you characterize the tone that the interviewer and interviewee had?
  ◇ Did the rhythm or pace of the interview affect the outcome? Why or why not?
  ◇ What was the hardest question for the interviewee to answer? Why?

- Watch an episode of a television show where an interview occurred. Identify two open, two closed, and two leading questions. Also, identify two question problems that occurred during the interview.

- Imagine that you are interviewing the Governor of your state about why funding for higher education is being cut in the budget. (This issue, of course, affects your tuition and funding for school). Construct five primary questions and five secondary/probing questions. Write five different kinds of probing/secondary questions. The probing/secondary questions should be indented under the primary question.

- If you could interview a famous person and were only allowed to ask five questions of this person, whom would you interview and what would you ask? Why would you ask these questions?

d i s c u s s i o n   q u e s t i o n s

- ◆ Which type of question do you think is the hardest to answer? Why?
- ◆ What is the purpose of asking questions in an interview?
- ◆ How do you think poorly worded questions affect the interviewee's response during an interview?
- ◆ Do you think loaded questions affect responses received? How?
- ◆ How important is courage during an interview?
- ◆ What types of confidentiality issues exist when questioning another individual?
- ◆ How long is too long to wait to answer a question?
- ◆ How powerful do you believe questions to be?
- ◆ How, as an interviewer, do you uncover information during an interview without trapping someone?
- ◆ How is questioning someone different than cross-examining someone?

QUESTIONS & THEIR PROBLEMS

Questions are tools and you can make a mistake without realizing it. If you have to develop questions on the spot it is easy to make mistakes.

Problem	Description/Definition	Example	How to avoid it
Only One Answer	Ask a yes/no question when more detail or specific detail needed.	Did you like school? Are you familiar with WIU? Do you know what happened next?	Use only when want /need single word reply. Avoid starting questions with do, can, have, would, will. Start questions with: Explain, what, how, tell me.
Keep Asking	Ask an open question and continue asking questions before respondent can answer.	What did you do next? Did you call security?	Stop asking after the first open question. Think through and prepare questions in advance of the interview.
Combined Question	Ask more than one question at a time.	What are your goals, aspirations, and where do you plan to be in five years?	Separate questions; ask only one at a time.
Leading	Answer is suggested in the question.	I love politics, don't you?	Make questions neutral. Only use leading questions when needed.
The Guess	Guess for answer rather than ask.	Would you call that fair? Were you first on the list?	Ask open questions.
Unnecessary	Question that is not necessary. Usually has an obvious answer.	Do you want your children to be healthy?	Think before asking.

Asking Effective Questions

Below, and on the following page, you will find two interview question schedules. Look over both schedules and determine which one is more effective. Why is it more effective?

Sample Schedule 1

Purpose: You have decided to interview Ms. Samantha Palmer. Ms. Palmer is the Director of Marketing at a well-known public relations firm in Cleveland, Ohio. Your goal is to learn as much as you can about the duties and responsibilities of her position. Your future career goal is to work in the public relations area.

Ms. Palmer, I am interested in a future career in the public relations field. Please tell me how you prepared to enter this field.

> What is the highest degree of education you have?
>
> What experience did you have prior to entering this career field?
>
> What was the first position you held in the public relations field?

What qualifications should one possess prior to entering the public relations career field?

What is a typical day like for you?

> How many hours per week do you work?
>
> What percent of time is spent on the telephone?
>
> What percent of time is spent at your desk on bookwork, or paperwork?
>
> What is the most challenging part of your job?
>
> What do you like the most about your job?
>
> What do you like the least about your job?
>
> What is the most frustrating part of your job?
>
> What problems do you face every day?

How do you prepare for your job each day?

Sample Schedule 2

Purpose: You have decided to interview Ms. Samantha Palmer. Ms. Palmer is the Director of Marketing at a well-known public relations firm in Cleveland, Ohio. Your goal is to learn as much as you can about the duties and responsibilities of her position. Your future career goal is to work in the public relations area.

Ms. Palmer, I am interested in a future career in the public relations field. Can you tell me how you prepared to enter this field?

> Do you have a master's degree?

> What did you major in during college?

> Did you work in the public relations field before accepting your current position?

What qualifications did you have prior to entering the public relations field?

Can you describe what a typical day is like for you?

> Do you travel a lot?

> Do you supervise anyone?

> What are your daily problems, responsibilities, and duties?

> Is time management important at your job?

Informational Interview Experience

For this assignment you will participate in an Informational Interview. You will gain practice writing effective questions, providing probing/secondary questions, and listening.

The first thing you need to do is to list five of the most frustrating things about the campus you attend or the things that bother you the most about the campus. If you are totally pleased with your campus and have no frustrations, list five things that you are curious about on campus.

Share these frustrations with the entire class while the professor or another student lists them on the board. As a class decide on the top three frustrations on campus. This can be determined by discussion or a vote. From the top three, choose one that affects college students/college life the most.

As a class, determine the goal(s) of the interview. What would you like to know about this topic? With your professor, decide who you need to interview in order to learn as much as you can about this topic. The professor will contact this individual(s) and invite him/her/them to a future class.

After the professor has secured a date for the interview it is now time to research this topic, the interviewee, and prepare a list of questions. Discuss the research that needs to be conducted prior to the interview as well as where to conduct this research (campus web site, brochures, public relations, school archives, etc.).

Between now and the next class period conduct research and bring your findings to class. Share your findings with the class and as a class decide on the topics that need to be covered during the interview.

In a group of four students choose one of the topic areas and prepare a list of questions along with possible probing/secondary questions. Turn this list of questions in and the professor will copy these and distribute to the entire class next class period. During the next class period, as a class, prepare the final schedule of questions.

On the day of the interview, each group will be responsible for asking the questions in their topic area. One group should be responsible for both the opening and the closing of the interview.

During the course of the interview pay attention to the following:

- How well did the questions your group prepared elicit the information that you wanted?
- How could your questions be improved?
- What further questions would you like to ask this individual(s) about this topic?
- While listening to questions from other groups, make note of the questions that worked well and the questions that had problems. How could questions from other groups be improved?
- After the interview, look over the notes you took during the interview. Are you able to recall and remember information from the interview based on your notes?
- How can you improve your note taking skills for future interviews?

Sample Situations

Please create interview questions for some sample occupations/situations. You will need to write six different types of questions, which include: open, closed, secondary/probing, neutral, threatening, and leading.

1. A professional baseball player whose team just won the World Series.

   Open:

   Closed:

   Secondary/Probing:

   Neutral:

   Threatening:

   Leading:

2. A chef in an Italian restaurant.

   Open:

   Closed:

   Secondary/Probing:

   Neutral:

   Threatening:

   Leading:

3. A student who was just elected as a state delegate to the National Green Party Convention.

   Open:

   Closed:

   Secondary/Probing:

   Neutral:

   Threatening:

   Leading:

4. A model for a popular brand of make-up.

   Open:

   Closed:

   Secondary/Probing:

   Neutral:

   Threatening:

   Leading:

5. A member of Cirque de Soleil.

   Open:

   Closed:

   Secondary/Probing:

   Neutral:

   Threatening:

   Leading:

Name _____ Date _____

Sample Situations *continued*

6. A fellow student who just returned from a tour in Afghanistan.

   Open:

   Closed:

   Secondary/Probing:

   Neutral:

   Threatening:

   Leading:

7. The producer of an academy award winning film.

   Open:

   Closed:

   Secondary/Probing:

   Neutral:

   Threatening:

   Leading:

8. The owner of a day spa and salon.

   Open:

   Closed:

   Secondary/Probing:

   Neutral:

   Threatening:

   Leading:

9. The coach of a collegiate basketball team.

   Open:

   Closed:

   Secondary/Probing:

   Neutral:

   Threatening:

   Leading:

10. A penguin animal trainer.

   Open:

   Closed:

   Secondary/Probing:

   Neutral:

   Threatening:

   Leading:

Sample Situations *continued*

11. The owner of a New York-based bridal store.

   Open:

   Closed:

   Secondary/Probing:

   Neutral:

   Threatening:

   Leading:

12. A doctor who recently lost his medical license.

   Open:

   Closed:

   Secondary/Probing:

   Neutral:

   Threatening:

   Leading:

Question Exercise

1. Imagine you are the reporter for the University newspaper. You have just arrived on the scene of a fire in the University Union/Student Center. There are several bystanders and two police officers on the scene. You decide to interview one of the police officers. List below three primary open questions you can ask to get information about this incident.

2. Identify each of the following questions in three ways (1) open or closed, (2) primary or secondary, (3) neutral or leading.
   a. Why do you say that?

   b. On a scale of one to five, with five being high, how would you rate the football coach?

   c. Tell me about your field trip to Montana?

   d. Do you want to give *that much* to the Salvation Army?

   e. What else do I need to know about the crime scene?

3. Identify the problems in the following questions. Rephrase each question to make it a good question. Avoid a problem question in your revised question. Don't change the original question.

a. Tell me about the fire. Was it scary?

b. You are going to vote, aren't you?

c. Do you want to fail this course?

d. (Asked by a doctor) Did your back begin to give you trouble after the hockey game?

e. (Asked of a McDonald's manager) Do you think McDonald's burgers are the best in the fast food business?

f. How are the lectures and the readings in this course?

g. Do you like this university because of the choice in majors?

Gaining Information through Effective Questioning

Below are several questions that may be asked during an interview. Beneath each question is an insufficient answer from the interviewee. Write the next secondary/probing question you would ask if you were the interviewer to obtain further information.

1. Question: Tell me what happened here.
   Answer: There was a fire.
   Your next question:

2. Question: Tell me about your recent win at the tournament.
   Answer: It was awesome.
   Your next question:

3. Question: Who do you admire the most?
   Answer: I don't know.
   Your next question:

4. Question: Tell me about a time when you showed your greatest strength.
   Answer: I think I am a very dedicated and loyal person.
   Your next question:

5. Question: What is your favorite hobby?
   Answer: When I was a kid I loved to horseback ride.
   Your next question:

6. Question: How do you react when everything seems to go wrong?
   Answer: I have days like that often.
   Your next question:

Interview Question Critique

Choose an interview on the internet or television to watch. It will be beneficial to record this interview because you may want to replay the interview several times to answer the questions for this assignment. Make sure the interview you choose is at least eight minutes long. After you have watched the interview, answer the following questions. Remember, you may need to replay the interview several times in order to effectively provide answers to all of the questions.

1. Who was the interviewer and the interviewee? _____

   _____

2. What was the goal/purpose of the interview? _____

   _____

3. List three effective questions that you heard during the interview. _____

   _____

   _____

   _____

4. List two ineffective questions that you heard during the interview. _____

   _____

   _____

   _____

5. In what ways could these questions be improved? Rewrite the questions in the space below.

_____

_____

_____

6. How could the interviewer improve the interview? _____

_____

7. How could the interviewee improve the interview? _____

_____

_____

Writing and Asking Effective Questions

The following are questions which do not follow the rules for effective questions. Identify the problem with each question and rewrite the question to make it an effective question. Make sure to include probing/secondary questions when necessary.

1. What is your major and why did you choose that major?

2. Name a place you would like to travel to and why?

3. Are you disgusted with the nation's economy like most U.S. citizens?

4. Do you plan on graduating any time in the near future?

5. Do you have a specific career in mind?

6. What specific goals do you have in mind for yourself (personally) in the next five years, ten years?

7. Do you consider yourself to be a more spontaneous or goal driven person?

8. Are children more influenced by media or parents and why?

9. Are you a leader or a follower?

10. Does your minor pertain to your major choice?

Teaching Effective Questioning Skills

Imagine your friend has just learned that you have completed a section on effective questioning in your interviewing class. Your friend is president of an organization that is getting ready to interview new applicants for membership into their group. Your friend has asked you to attend the group's meeting and give a presentation. You have also been asked to prepare a one page tip sheet on preparing and asking effective questions. Prepare this tip sheet based on what you have learned in class and from your text regarding preparing and asking effective questions. Make sure you have at least twelve tips and several examples on your tip sheet.

Image © More Images, 2012. Used under license from Shutterstock, Inc.

e x e r c i s e s

◆ Watch an interview. During the opening of the interview, try to identify how one party works to establish rapport with the other party.

   ◇ Was there a form of ritualistic greeting? If yes, describe.

   ◇ Did one party try to show some type of care/concern for the other individual? If so, how?

   ◇ Was disclosure part of this interview?

   ◇ Write a reaction to this interview and include how these above items worked to create rapport and/or how their absence worked against the individuals in the interview. What could the parties have done to better their rapport?

◆ Go to a local mall, store, or business where you may be approached by an interviewer wanting you to complete a survey or a sales associate attempting to sell you something. Pay special attention to how they open the interview with you. Based on what you have learned about interview openings, write a one page response paper addressing how this opening could be improved.

♦ Recall a time when you received a phone call asking you to complete a survey over the phone. How did the interviewer open the interview? How did the interviewer close the interview? Did you complete the survey? Why or why not? If you were the interviewer working for this same company, how would you convince respondents to participate in your survey? How would you open your interview? What do you think some of the problems are with telephone interviews? What are the benefits of telephone interviews?

♦ Think about a time when you've had people over to your home. How do you greet guests? What do you say? What do you do? How can you parallel your "home" experiences to those in an interview (regardless of the type)?

♦ Make a list of ten primary questions that are all closed. Next, turn those ten primary questions into ten primary open questions. Finally, arrange those into a schedule.

♦ In class, pair up with another student. Create a guide about the following: information related to interviewing, type of future career goals, current semester interests, summer plans, hobbies, miscellaneous interests, etc. Turn your guide into a schedule of questions using one of the question sequences. Next, interview your partner (and let your partner interview you) following one of the question sequences (tunnel, funnel, inverted funnel, hourglass, diamond, parallel, quintamensional, or chain-link). Why did you choose the sequence you did? Was it effective? How could you tell?

♦ Keep a log (for a week) of every instance where someone interviewed you. After each interview, note the following:
   ◇ Type of interview
   ◇ Opening and closing techniques
   ◇ Nonverbals during the interview
   ◇ Questions (What kind were they? What did you like? What didn't you like?)

♦ Suppose you had the opportunity to interview someone famous. First, come up with a guide of topics that you would want to interview this person about. Second, take the guide and create a schedule of questions. Be sure to include headings, transitions, and at least 15 primary questions (with 15 possible secondary/probing questions). Don't forget to put the goal/purpose at the top.

♦ In class, get into groups of four people. Next, as a group decide who (famous/not-famous) you would want to interview (all four people have to agree). Second, in your group of four, come up with a guide of topics for this interview. Third, two group members choose a question sequence and write out a schedule for that person. The remaining two group members choose a different question sequence and write out a schedule for that famous/not-famous person. Fourth, compare the two schedules. Which do you think is most effective? Why?

♦ Find what you consider to be an example of either a "good/complete" opening or closing or a "bad/incomplete" opening or closing and bring to class.
   ◇ Choose one (not your own) interview to watch from those shared by your classmates and critique what made it a "good/complete" or a "bad/incomplete" interview. Discuss your findings in a one page response paper.

- Read through a career and informational gathering interviewing assignment. You need to narrow down the individual that you plan to interview. Start thinking about the topics/information that you would like to discover from this individual. Prepare a guide of topics and turn that into your first draft of a schedule. Make sure to include a purpose statement (what is your overall goal for this interview). Turn in your guide and schedule for completion of this assignment.
- Watch an interview (either on television or online). Try to identify the following components:
  ◇ Purpose
  ◇ Opening Techniques
  ◇ Question Sequence
  ◇ Problem Questions
  ◇ Closing Techniques
  ◇ Types of secondary questions/probes

discussion questions

- Why does an interview have to have a goal?
- Most of us have watched or witnessed an interview in which the interviewer fails to use an appropriate opening or closing. How does this lack of either an opening/closing affect the interview climate and the parties involved? Describe in detail and be specific.
- Discuss an instance when you met someone for the very first time and a negative impression was made. What occurred during the opening of this interaction to make it a lasting negative impression? Describe in detail.
- How important are rapport and orientation during an interview? Explain.
- Name five things that you would consider a "no-no" to do during an interview.
- How much influence do you believe the opening of an interview has on the information exchanged during the body of the interview?
- How might different types of interviews require a different type of structure? Or do they?
- How might what you say/do in the first few minutes of an interview have an influence on how the other party perceives you (and the particulars of that situation)?
- How can an opening determine whether an interview will continue or end?
- Some say the opening of an interview is like a game of chess. Why would this comparison be made?
- How can you work to establish good rapport? Bad rapport?
- What do you think rapport consists of?
- Is small talk important during the opening of an interview? Why or why not?
- What does uncertainty reduction have to do with interviewing?
- Do nonverbal signals play a role in the opening techniques of an interview? Body? Closing?
- How important is dress to the opening (and success) of an interview?
- What is the difference between interview schedules?

Opening Scenarios

Below are opening scenarios. Read through each opening and determine what needs to be adjusted in order to make each opening effective.

Scenario 1: This is a persuasive interview between Mary who is looking for a new car and Randy a car salesman.

> Interviewer: Hello, my name is Randy (shakes hands with interviewee). How can I help you today?
>
> Interviewee: Introduces self (shakes hands with interviewer). I am looking for a more economical car to drive to work.
>
> Interviewer: We have several late model cars at the back of the lot.

Scenario 2: This is a selection interview at a small department store in the mall.

> Interviewer: Hello, welcome to Jingle's Department Store. I hope you found my office okay.
>
> Interviewee: Yes, I walked right to it.
>
> Interviewer: Please make yourself comfortable and let's get started with the interview. Tell me about yourself.

Scenario 3: This is an information gathering interview between a reporter for the lifestyle section of the local newspaper and a new business that just opened in town.

> Interviewer: Hello, my name is Ginger. I am the reporter for the local newspaper.
>
> Interviewee: Hello.
>
> Interviewer: Since you have opened your business, have you been successful?

Scenario 4: This is an interview between a student and professor.

> Interviewer: (Knocks on professor's office door) Hi Professor Smith, I need to talk to you.
>
> Interviewee: I have class in five minutes.
>
> Interviewer: This will only take a couple of minutes. Yesterday in class you said . . . .

Closing Scenarios

Below are closing scenarios. Read through each closing and determine what needs to be adjusted in order to make each closing effective.

Scenario 1: This is a Helping Interview between Darryl and his counselor.

> Interviewer: I think you are making great progress. I have another appointment.
>
> Interviewee: Thanks. I appreciate your help with my problem.
>
> Interviewer: I'm glad I could help you. Do you think you can continue on your current path?

Scenario 2: This is a Persuasive Interview between Stacey and David.

> Interviewer: Like I said, this is the best deal on the home entertainment system that you will find.
>
> Interviewee: I am just starting to look for a system. I really like this one.
>
> Interviewer: Well, when you make up your mind just let me know.
>
> Interviewee: Thanks.

Scenario 3: This is an Information Gathering Interview between a television reporter and a family who lost their home in a tornado.

> Interviewer: When the tornado slammed into your home what did you do?
>
> Interviewee: (very emotional) We took cover in the basement.
>
> Interviewer: Wow. I see the rescue workers approaching. Let's see what they have to say.

Scenario 4: This is a performance review of John Robinson who has been on probation because of too many absences.

> Interviewer: Your attendance has been better these last few weeks.
>
> Interviewee: I have been trying to get my life straightened out. It is really hard. I don't know how long I can keep going like this.
>
> Interviewer: Well, keep up the good attendance. That is all.

Schedule Preparation

Following are several questions for a "get to know your classmate" interview. Arrange these questions into a moderate schedule with a purpose statement which includes your goal. Include topic headings, probing questions and place transitions between each topic section. Make sure to rewrite unclear and ineffective questions.

What is your favorite thing about college?

What is your major and why did you choose that major?

What is your dream job and why?

What high school did you graduate from and when?

What type of career do you see yourself doing once you graduate?

Who is the biggest influence in your life and why?

Do you plan on graduating any time in the near future?

If you had six months left to live what would you do with your time?

What made you decide that you wanted a career in a specific field?

What is your greatest accomplishment up to this point in your life?

What is the best job that you have had so far and why?

What specific goals do you have in mind for yourself personally in the next five years and ten years?

What is a major problem you faced in one of your jobs?

How did you overcome that problem?

What is your hometown?

Tell me about a problem you had with a supervisor?

What are your strengths?

What are things you look for in a real job?

What is your minor?

Does your minor pertain to your major choice?

What is your name?

Question Sequence Scenarios

Below are a number of interviewing scenarios. Determine which question sequence would be the most effective in order to encourage the interviewee to reveal information and talk during the interview.

1. Jillian is administering a survey in order to determine how respondents feel about the university's plans to build a new dining hall in the center of campus.

2. Steven is an attorney and must interview a client who was involved in an accident eighteen months ago. Steven knows this client may have a hard time remembering details of the accident and that some of the memories may be difficult for the client to talk about.

3. Richard is a reporter for the local television station. He is attending a community meeting at the local high school where community residents plan to discuss the consolidation of their school district and the school district in the neighboring town. Richard knows that several residents in the town have very strong feelings regarding this consolidation possibility and they are ready and willing to share their views.

4. Scott is an investigator for the Illinois State Police. He is interviewing a reticent and uncooperative suspect who has been brought in for questioning.

5. Niko is conducting research to determine the opinions of his respondents.

6. Kaylee and Eddie are consultants who have been hired by the Bytine Manufacturing Company to conduct interviews with their employees in order to determine the most important training needs. The employees have been asking for additional training for several months and are excited that their concerns have been heard by the managers.

Sequence Identification

Below are question sequences. Identify each question sequence.

Tell me about your career search.

What has been your most interesting interview experience?

In what geographical area are you conducting your search?

How many interviews have you had?

Have you received any job offers?

_____

What happened here?

How did this fire start?

How much damage has this fire caused?

How many fire crews are on the scene?

What time did the fire department receive the 911 call?

_____

Did you attend the meeting?

Approximately how many people attended the meeting?

How do you feel about the meeting?

What was discussed at the meeting?

_____

What do you know about the administrator's decision to build another dining hall?

How would a new dining hall benefit you?

Do you believe a new dining hall is needed?

Tell me why you feel this way?

_____

Tell me about your spring break trip.

Which states did you visit?

Which was your favorite?

Do you plan to return to this state?

5

Framing

Image © Hannamariah, 2012. Used under license from Shutterstock, Inc.

e x e r c i s e s

♦ Imagine you are a reporter for a major news outlet. You have recently been assigned a major story which could propel you up the chain of command and possibly even win you some awards. However, gathering information could be difficult given the subject matter. You will have to establish rapport and gain information with those you come into contact with (not to mention establish credibility). Your job is to think of how you can reframe the situation (maybe even the environment) so as to make individuals feel comfortable enough with you to grant you the interview.

◇ Are there interviewing situations where changing the frame could help the interviewer gain more information?

- What would the location be?
- Describe the environment.
- What would you be doing?
- What would you be saying?

- Locate an interview where you feel framing became a major focus. What occurred during this interview? How did the frame at the beginning of the interview change by the end of the interview?

- Find three examples of how the media covered the BP Oil Spill of 2010. You will need to locate three examples from 2010 and then three examples from 2011.
    ◇ Write a one page response and include these ideas:
        • What type of sources did you find to read about the oil spill (for both time periods)?
        • How did these sources frame this event?
            ◦ Was the coverage different? If yes, why.
        • What did you learn about the spill?
        • How did framing play a role in this event?

- Read or watch a clip of Abbott and Costello's "Who's on First?"
    ◇ What occurred during this clip (or transcript)?
    ◇ How is this an example of framing?

- How would you frame the following scenarios:
    ◇ A student received a poor grade on an exam in class. He needs to talk to the professor about the implications of this on his grade.
        • How would the student frame this interaction?
        • How would the professor frame this interaction?

- During class, pair up with another student. Watch an interview (played by your professor) during class. Do not take notes during the playing of the interview. After the interview is over, talk about your observations (frames) of the interview. Discuss:
    ◇ Your perceptions of the tone of the interview.
        • Was he/she excited to be interviewed? Bored? Preoccupied with nitpicking the questions, etc.?
    ◇ Any striking quotations (short or long) that you remembered with confidence?
        • Why did you remember these quotes?
    ◇ What important pieces of information did you take note that aided the purpose/goal of the interview?
    ◇ How were your observations different, similar, etc.?
    ◇ Why is a perception/framing check important to take note of?

- Create a metaphor to the concept of framing.
    ◇ Why did you create this metaphor?
    ◇ How is it similar to framing?
    ◇ How is it different?

discussion questions

- How do you describe framing?
- How does framing help create meaning?
- How does word choice affect whether something is framed in a particular way?
- In what situations should we engage in framing? Explain.
- How does one's role play a part in framing?
- Discuss a real situation in which framing became, or was essentially, very important to the outcome of an interaction.
- Do you feel people often misuse the concept of framing? If so, how? Provide an example.
- How might contextualizing a situation help in the concept of framing?
- Think of a situation you were involved in which resulted in a misunderstanding or miscommunication. Explain the situation. Then, explain if and how framing the situation (and/or framing questions) would have helped the situation.
- Can framing be compared to punctuation? If yes, how?
- How important is tone to the concept of framing?
- Do you think men and women frame differently? If yes, describe.
- Do you think the media frames issues? If so, how? Provide an example.
- Does the media's frame of an issue impact public opinion of an issue, person, event, or idea? If yes, explain.
- Do counselors use the concept of framing (Helping Interview)? If yes, describe how.
- Is framing more important in social situations or in interviewing situations? Explain.

Framing Practice

When interviewing it is necessary to understand that not all people will have the same perspective or interpret an event, situation, or happening the same way. Using effective framing will help individuals correctly interpret what is going on in situations. Determining the meaning of communication in relation to the context is what framing is all about.

Consider the following scenario.

Mr. Elmer Smith was an 80-year-old retired real estate broker from a small town in west central Illinois. Mr. Smith recently suffered a fatal massive stroke. Mr. Smith was quite wealthy and rumor has it he has left much of his estate to local charities while leaving little or nothing to his estranged children and grandchildren. Mr. Smith's attorney has scheduled a meeting with Mr. Smith's children, Doug, Darren, and Darlene to discuss the provisions of their father's will. Also present at this reading of the will are the directors of several local charities including the local food bank, churches, Red Cross, and Salvation Army.

After the reading of the will Mr. Smith's children have agreed to have an interview with you, the reporter for the local newspaper, regarding the distribution of their father's fortune. Prepare a moderate interview schedule including a variety of frames for this interview. Include at least ten primary questions with frames and ten possible secondary/probing questions.

Now, imagine you have the opportunity to interview the local charity that received the majority of Mr. Smith's estate. Prepare a moderate interview schedule including a variety of frames. Include at least ten primary questions with frames and ten possible probing questions.

International Interview Assignment

For this assignment, you will interview a person from another culture. This may be a person who previously lived in another country/culture and now resides in the United States. This may also be a person who is living in the United States for a short time but is a citizen of another country, such as an international student.

Your goal for this assignment is to learn as much as you can about another culture from an individual who has lived in that culture. You will also practice the skills of listening, note taking, and maintaining eye contact while interviewing another individual.

Our view of reality is shaped by our culture. We see and interpret the world through our lenses or our own frame. No two people share the exact same frame. Different cultures have different ways of interacting and showing respect. For example, in the North American culture speakers expect listeners will make eye contact with them and listeners are also expected to give nonverbal encouragers to indicate recognition and listening. In the North American culture, individuals should maintain a distance of about one arm's length, or four feet, during a social conversation and common courtesies such as shaking hands when meeting and holding the door open for someone are expected. These expectations and rules/courtesies may be foreign to members of another culture.

You must decide what background information you need in order to prepare an effective list of questions and have a successful interview. For example, you may want to research the location, climate, and origins of the country/culture. Conduct research and prepare a schedule (list) of questions. Make sure to include possible secondary/probing questions on your list of questions.

You will want to include questions about behaviors, customs, and traditions that may affect interviews (for example, gender differences/expectations, verbal and nonverbal behaviors, shared and understood values in the culture, approach to conflict, etc.). Also make sure to ask the interviewee to compare and contrast the United States culture to their home culture.

Schedule a meeting with the person you plan to interview. Make sure to meet with your international partner in a public place, such as the library, student common area, coffee shop, etc. During this interview you will need to use effective listening, note taking, and eye contact. While taking notes write only key words that will help you remember the information being provided. Do not write full sentences.

Upon completion of this interview write a four to five page paper describing your research and what you learned from your partner.

Question Frames

Scenario: You have worked in the public relations department at the local community hospital for the past seven years, and have managed the office for the past three years. You manage two full-time and one part-time staff members. Your office is responsible for all publication materials concerning the hospital/staff and all the press releases. All the staff members in your department are efficient, competent, and show initiative on all projects. However, because of the heavy work-load, the office has a need for another full-time position. For years, you have requested a full-time assistant director position for your office. Recently, the CEO of the hospital has advised you that the position request has finally been approved by the Board of Directors.

For the past three months, one of your full-time staff members, Rhonda Smith has missed the deadlines for the monthly newsletter and has been late to work several times, plus missed more days than usual due to illness. The other full-time staff member, Joel Martin has been covering for Rhonda and filling in as needed. Since the Public Relations Office is a very stressful office and extremely busy, the absence of one staff member is noticed and the strain of the extra work is starting to influence the office morale and work.

You must call Rhonda into your office and talk to her concerning her performance.

Write the following frames to use during this interview:

1. Frame to recognize efforts or qualifications:

2. Frame to reduce the threat of the question/save face:

3. Frame to provide facts:

Framing Questions

Consider each of the following scenarios. In the space below each scenario write a question using a frame.

1. You want to ask the guest speaker at a college medical symposium about AIDS but think it might be ego threatening.

   _____

   _____

   _____

2. You have heard it is very difficult for women to be accepted as equal partners in certain medical practices and want to ask a female partner in a medical practice what her experience has been. You realize this may be personal and subjective based on her experiences only.

   _____

   _____

   _____

3. Your goal is to start your own business, so you have decided to interview a self-employed individual. You have read that two out of three small businesses fail within the first three years. You are afraid some of your questions might be too personal but you really want to ask them.

   _____

   _____

   _____

4. You would like to ask an acquaintance who has recently been hired into an entry level position in a career field you are interested in, about their salary.

_____

_____

_____

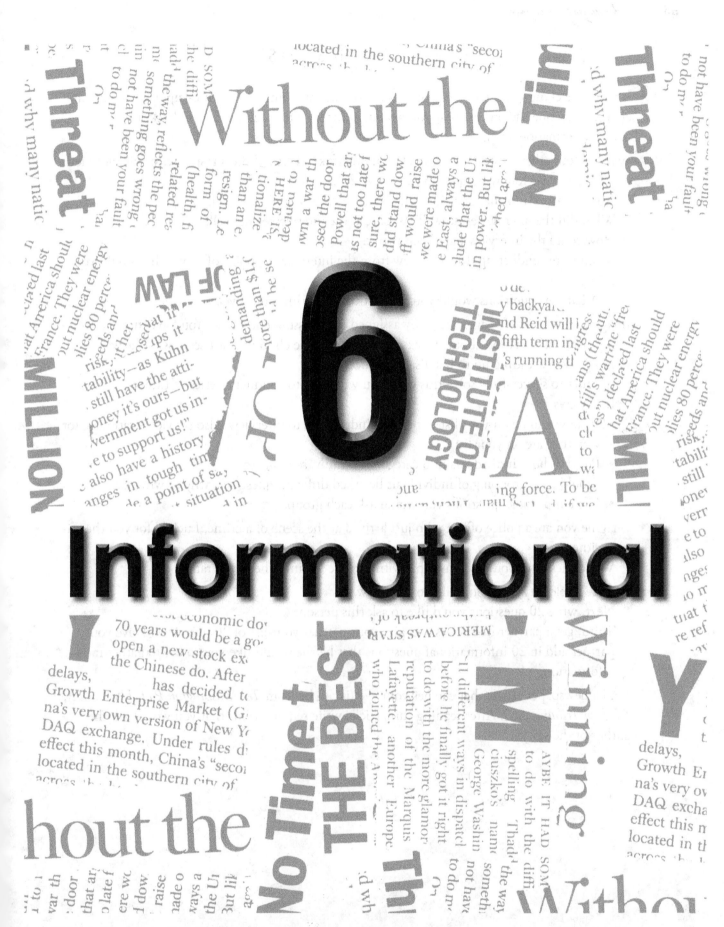

e x e r c i s e s

- If you were chosen to interview a famous band that was coming to your campus for a musical concert, describe the process that you would go through to interview them (background, question formation, etc.).

- Watch a Journalistic Interview on television (and take notes). Write a response to this interview by answering the following questions:
  ◇ What type of Informational Interview was this? How could you tell?
  ◇ What did the interviewer do well? What did the interviewee do well?
  ◇ How could the interview have been better?
  ◇ If you were conducting this interview from the interviewer's point of view, what would you change?
    • What new questions would you ask (list between three and five).

- Imagine you are an FBI agent recently assigned to a missing child case. You have minimal background information about the case so far (where the child was last seen, what he was wearing, events leading up to his disappearance, etc.)
  ◇ In order to successfully solve this case, you will need to conduct a series of Informational Interviews.
    • Who would be on your list of possible individuals to interview (also provide a rationale for why they are on your list)?
    • Put the above individuals into categories (family, school, etc.).
    • Would each grouping of individuals be asked different questions, why or why not?
    • List ten possible questions you would ask each group.

- Imagine you are a police officer who just arrived at the scene of a crime. Luckily for you there is one witness.
  ◇ What questions would you ask this witness? The victim? The perpetrators?

- Choose a celebrity that you'd like to interview.
  ◇ Next, write 20 questions you'd like to ask this person.
  ◇ Third, get a partner from class and give your partner your list of 20 questions. Have your partner add in 20 informational questions that he/she would like you to use to gather more information.

- Find a newspaper article that catches your eye (it can be from *The Washington Post, USA Today, Chicago Tribune,* etc.). After reading this article, write ten questions that you would ask the author of the story.

d i s c u s s i o n   q u e s t i o n s

- What are the various types of Informational Interviews?

- How important is the medium during an Informational Interview? Why?

- What do you think are challenges for interviewers before going into an Informational Interview?

- How can Informational Interviews be deceitful?

- What types of questions do you think that interviewer should avoid during an Informational Interview? Why?

- Does an Informational Interview need to last long to be effective? Why or why not.

- Discuss an instance in your life when you have had to probe another individual to get information.

- Probing often involves delving into personal feelings and emotions. How do you respond to a probing question when you really don't feel like expressing your emotions/feelings?

- As an interviewer you must motivate an interviewee to disclose beliefs, attitudes, and feelings as well as unknown facts. What ideas do you have to motivate an interviewee?

- What ideas do you have for improving how you ask questions during an Informational Interview to get the information you want?

- Are there ethical guidelines to consider during an Informational Interview? If so, name and describe a few.

- How do listening and note-taking play a role in an Informational Interview?

- During an interview situation, an interviewer may encounter a difficult interviewee. Think of an interview you have been involved in or witnessed in which there was a difficult interviewee. How did this affect the interview? How did the interviewer handle the interviewee? What could the interviewer have done differently?

Truth Behind the Tale

Objective: To provide you with an opportunity to practice interviewing concepts discussed throughout the course.

Rationale: This exercise gives you an opportunity to practice a multitude of interviewing concepts/techniques, which are valuable in a variety of settings. First, this activity gives you practice writing interviewing questions (open, closed, primary, secondary, neutral, and leading). Second, you will have extended practice at an Informational Interview.

Time for Activity: 75 minutes

Resources Needed: Copies of various fairy tales. There are numerous places where you can locate fairy tales. A few (non-book) suggested websites include: http://hca.gilead.org.il/#list, http://onlinebooks.library.upenn.edu/webbin/book/browse?type=lcsubc&key=Fairy%20tales, http://www.familymanagement.com/literacy/grimms/grimms-toc.html and www.grimmfairytales.com.

Activity: Class Period #1—Choose a group of other students to pair up with for this activity. Ideally, you must find at least two partners and choose a fairy tale. (Each group will need to find a fairy tale containing the same number of main characters as members of the group). You will then "become" one of the main characters in the fairy tale. As this character, you will be responsible for putting thought into what events occurred during the tale and also what resulted (or could have resulted) from the tale (possibly even what the aftermath of the tale was along with any consequences). After reflecting on the aforementioned ideas, you must write at least six primary questions to ask each of the other characters.

Class Period #2—You should gather with the other members of your group (and have your schedule of questions). Each group member will now take on three roles throughout this exercise (interviewer, interviewee, and observer).

During the exercise, you should interview the other characters (one at a time), be interviewed, and observe the other characters interviewing one another.

After the activity is over, you should do one of the following:

1. Submit a write up of your experiences and include what occurred during the duration of the interview (reflecting on all three roles).
2. After the interviews are over, peer critique your fellow group members/characters and the questions that were asked (question construction, question problems, etc.).
3. Turn in the schedule of questions for points and have the questions labeled as open, closed, loaded, etc.).
4. To enhance the experience, this exercise could be lengthened so that you create an opening and a closing for the other characters during the interview.
5. A variation of this exercise could include a panel interview. So, instead of having one-on-one character interviews, two (or more depending on group size) group members/characters could panel interview other members of the group.
6. Write a paper reflecting on the probing skills used, note-taking, elements of verbal and nonverbal communication you believe influenced the interactions during the interview, listening approaches, and other elements.

Interview of a Murderer?

Purpose: To practice interviewing questions (i.e., open/closed, primary/secondary, neutral/leading), guides/schedules, and informational interviewing.

Objectives:

- Your professor will provide you with a murder mystery character (background and secret information). This should not be shared with anyone (no exceptions).

- You are to become one with your character. Truly try to get into the mindset of who your character is and what your character must accomplish throughout the next class period. During the next class period you and your fellow students will become part of a murder mystery event.

- Before the next class, you are to create an interview guide and schedule. The overall goal of the murder mystery is to try and figure out "who" the murderer is. In order to do this, you will need to create a schedule of questions to ask the other characters. Come with a prepared schedule (typed). You should include a variety of questions (i.e., open/closed, primary/secondary, neutral/leading). Leave room on your schedule for probing questions you think to ask the characters as you interact with them.

- During the event, you must also create 10 additional questions which will be handwritten on the schedule.

Information:

- The class before the murder mystery event, you will be given a complete list of characters.

- The information you receive is very secretive—share this information with no one. The pink sheet reveals a lot of background information about your particular character. This should help guide you (in multiple ways).

- You must bring the blue sheet with you to class. This reveals to you what you must do at the murder mystery event. Every character has objectives they must complete. These will help give you clues as to who the murderer might be.

- Once you arrive to class, you will receive additional information and more objectives that must be completed.

- If you are the murderer or the one being killed—**TELL NO ONE**. The murder mystery will not be a success if you do!

- You should be selective as to whom you choose to share information with. Remember, you are trying to solve the murder *by whatever means necessary*. This may involve bribing (you will be given money), eavesdropping, manipulation, etc.

Good Luck and Have Fun!

Informational Interview

This is an opportunity to learn more about a topic you are curious about, while at the same time practice your Informational Interview preparation skills.

1. List topics that you would like to know more about. On your list you may include a hobby, vacation, sport, town, or an aspect of your future career. Choose one of these topics.
2. Narrow down what you would like to know about this topic. For example, if you would like to learn more about the country of Ireland, ask yourself specifically what would you like to know? Would you like to learn about the geography of Ireland, religion, customs and traditions, or the government of Ireland, etc.?
3. Conduct research on your topic and then develop an interview guide and schedule.
4. In order to answer the questions on your schedule determine who you should contact to complete this interview. Imagine that you can travel anywhere and time and money play no role in your decision of whom to interview. Choose the person or group of people you believe could provide you with the most current and correct information for this topic.
5. Type a two page response paper explaining the following:
   ♦ How important is research to the Informational Interview?
   ♦ Why is it important to prepare a schedule of questions for an Informational Interview?
   ♦ What factors should one consider when determining who to interview for an Informational Interview?
   ♦ Discuss what you learned about your topic from your research.

Your Dream Career

Imagine that you have just landed your dream career as a journalist for National Public Radio (NPR). Within your first year you are asked to go on assignment in Afghanistan. Your goal is to learn what a day is like for an American soldier fighting the War on Terror. You know that you should prepare for this interview by understanding as much as you can about the War on Terror. You have also been warned that you should be prepared to face difficult situations and conditions during this assignment. Based on this information, answer the following questions about your assignment.

How should you prepare for this interview?

What should your research include?

What conditions might you encounter in this setting?

How do you plan to handle these conditions?

What strategies would you employ while interviewing soldiers who are emotional?

What strategies would you employ while interviewing soldiers who are unwilling to talk?

What strategies would you employ while interviewing soldiers who insist on giving ambiguous or unclear answers to your questions?

7 Survey

Image © rangizzz, 2012. Used under license from Shutterstock, Inc.

e x e r c i s e s

- Generate a list of hot topics in the media right now that you might be interested in (do this in groups of three).
  - ◇ Each group will be assigned a different type of survey question. Your group needs to come up with 10 questions from your assigned category.

- Research the U.S. Census Bureau. Report your findings in a paper.
  - ◇ What is the most common type of question used?
  - ◇ How is the information gathered?
  - ◇ How are the findings reported?
  - ◇ How are the workers trained?

- Find a controversial issue on your campus at the moment. Research this issue with the intent of gaining more than enough information to develop a focus group about this particular issue.
  - ◇ Develop a focus group plan.
  - ◇ Who are the groups that need to be interviewed? Why?
  - ◇ What information do you want to gain?
  - ◇ How will the information be recorded?
  - ◇ Develop a guide/schedule for each constituency group.
    - • How are the questions alike?
    - • How are the questions different?

- If you and two classmates had to design a research project, discuss your proposal by answering the following questions in a paper:
  ◇ What is the goal of the project?
  ◇ Will you use qualitative vs. quantitative research?
  ◇ How will you select your interview subjects?
  ◇ What type of sampling will you use?
  ◇ What types of questions (and scale) will you ask?

- Get a copy of *The Chicago Tribune, USA Today, The Washington Post,* etc. Find an article that has a public opinion poll included. Discuss what this poll "said" about the topic it was reporting on.
  ◇ Was the audience of this poll discussed? If yes, who is the directed audience?
    • How many people were polled?
    • What is the geographic location of the audience?
  ◇ What is the margin of error?
  ◇ What types of questions were used?

- Imagine you are a campaign manager for a local state representative (rural area) and want to gather data about how the constituency feel in regard to school consolidations. Write a response to how you would gather data to answer this question.

- If you were a radio DJ and your station wanted to switch formats, how would you know which format to switch to?

- Think of a movie that has included scenes of a Survey Interview. Discuss the following in a one page paper:
  ◇ What type of Survey Interview was conducted?
  ◇ What types of questions were asked?
  ◇ Who was involved?

- Sign up to become a mystery shopper. As you walk through the store, ask for assistance from various employees. Ask about products, services, special ordering, location, and warranties, etc. After your interactions with the employees, write a paper about the following:
  ◇ What types of employee behavior did you notice?
    • What types of behavior did you think you would notice?
  ◇ What type of service did you receive? What type of service did other customers receive?
    • How many employees did you interact with?
    • What was consistent/inconsistent about their behavior?
    • What was consistent/inconsistent about their demeanor?
    • Did they have good product knowledge?
  ◇ How did you record your findings?
  ◇ Did anyone suspect that you were a mystery shopper?
    • If yes, why and how?

- Create a point of purchase interview project to be carried out by the end of the semester.
  ◇ What product would you focus on?
  ◇ At what location would this interview be held?
  ◇ Would interviewer bias play a role?

d i s c u s s i o n   q u e s t i o n s

- What do you think the overall purpose of doing a survey is?
- Which type of Survey Interview do you feel is the most effective? Why?
  ◇ Does the purpose of the interview play a role in your answer?
- What value does a pretest have in Survey Interviewing?
- Discuss the advantages and disadvantages of qualitative and quantitative interviews.
- Discuss how you would select interviewees for a survey.
- How does the opening and the closing for a Survey Interview differ from other types of interviews?
- If you had to give three tips to an interviewer conducting a Survey Interview, what would those be? Why?
- What role does the opening play in a Survey Interview?
- Describe reliability and consistency in terms of their importance in a Survey Interview.
- Have you ever been part of a focus group? If yes, discuss your experiences.
- What is the purpose of a focus group?
- If you had to describe the ideal training for someone conducting a Survey Interview, what would you include in this training?
- How accurate do you think exit polls are in a political campaign?
  ◇ When the media reports these polls, does it have the potential to influence someone who has yet to vote? Why or why not?
- Have you participated in a face-to-face or telephone survey? If so, describe how you felt while completing this survey. Did you feel it was beneficial or a waste of time?

Survey Scenario

Imagine that you serve on the city council for the small town in which you reside. The city council would like to improve the historic downtown area and thus decides to survey the residents of the town to determine their views on this improvement. Considering what you have learned about Survey Interviews, answer the following questions.

1. How can you get respondents to share and respond to your questions honestly?
2. What steps can you take to ensure that the respondents are answering accurately?
3. How can you encourage participation in your survey?
4. What are the advantages and disadvantages of the different types of survey instruments that can be used for this research?
5. How will you determine the objective/focus of this survey?
6. What type of data will this survey aim to gather?
7. What demographics should be taken into consideration?
8. How will you determine the sample for this survey?
9. What instructions will you provide to the respondents for this survey?
10. What types of questions should your survey include?

After you have answered the above questions, construct a survey for this city council research project.

Bring your survey to the next class period and compare your survey with those of your classmates.

The Survey Interview

Following are several questions from a survey. Read each question and determine the problem with each question. Rewrite each question.

1. What do you think of the recent proposal?

2. Do you agree that the mayor's response was uncalled for?

3. Is the entrance price fair?

4. How many times do you go to the gym?

5. Since you attended the "Vote No for School Consolidation" meeting you must be against school consolidation, correct?

6. Why do you dislike the presidential candidates?

"Was the interview too early for you?"

Image © Cartoonresource, 2012. Used under license from Shutterstock, Inc.

Recruiting

e x e r c i s e s

♦ Your university is hiring a new Communication professor. As a student, you have been selected to sit on the search committee. Create a list of basic skills you think this professor would need for this position.

♦ You have been asked by a colleague to write a recommendation letter. Your colleague is applying for a new position at another company. What would you include in this letter? What would you exclude?

◇ Write this letter.

- Attend a Career Fair. Talk to at least five different company recruiters to find out what types of skills they are looking for in recent college graduates.
  ◇ Write a response about what you found.
  ◇ Did anything surprise you? If yes, what?
  ◇ How do your traits match up with these skills?
  ◇ What do you need to improve upon?
- What do you think an entry level job pays?
  ◇ Search the web to find an entry level job description for the career that you seek.
  ◇ What did you notice? Is this more or less than you thought it would be?
  ◇ How does this affect your job search?
- Get into groups of four. As a group, you are now the "hiring committee" for your employer. Pick a position at your organization and pretend that you are now hiring for that position. First, list what the position is. Second, write the job description for what that employee does at your organization. Third, generate a list of the qualities that you would seek in a new employee. Fourth, construct a list of potential questions that you would ask individuals who would be interviewing for this position (include a variety of questions).
- Research the field that you are interested in. Figure out what some of the latest trends/fads, disappointments, developments, or legislation is in this field by finding four articles that relate to your field.
  ◇ Why is having this knowledge important?
- Find an article that relates to developing your "branding statement."
  ◇ Write a practice branding statement

discussion questions

- Do generations communicate differently?
  ◇ Why is this important when relating to interviews?
  ◇ What can we learn from the differences in generations?
- Has technology made recruiting easier or harder?
- As a potential employee, what should you look for in a company that you wish to interview at?
- How often do you believe that unlawful questions get asked?
- If you are asked to write a recommendation letter for someone, what would you want to make sure you included?
- What do you think are the first things that a recruiter would notice about a potential employee's resume?
- What is the most important thing that an applicant can do before entering into a Recruiting Interview? Why?
- How have societal changes altered the way individuals are recruited for potential jobs?
- Describe a Recruiting Interview that you have been on. What occurred? What was good about the interview? What was bad?

- Have you ever been a part of an interview where an Equal Employment Opportunity (EEO) law was broken? If so, describe the situation. How did you feel?

- Please share any experience you have had playing the role of the interviewer. Discuss how you prepared for the interview. Do you believe it was a successful interview? Why or why not?

- Discuss how important you believe preparing a position profile is to the success of a selection interview.

- Have you been involved in a situational interview as an interviewee? If so, share how it was different/similar to a traditional/standard interview.

- Do you think that people ever "trick" a recruiter during an Employment Interview? If so, how? Are there things that a recruiter can do to prevent this?

- How is your introduction (30–60 second commercial) like a television or radio sound bite? How is it different?

Recruiting Interview Preparation

As a recruiter, you have multiple decisions to make. Recruiting is a difficult, time consuming, and costly process. Prior to finding the best applicant to fill your open position, it is important to take the necessary steps to prepare. Below are some preparation steps needed.

1. Be aware of the Equal Employment Opportunity (EEO) laws and plan to comply with them.
2. Completely review and analyze the open position. This may include studying the job description and job shadowing the individual currently in this position. Determine the skills, characteristics, traits, abilities, education, knowledge, experience, training, etc. that the ideal candidate must possess. Make sure all of these are position related.
3. Based on the information you learned in number two above, write a position announcement.
4. Determine where to publicize your announcement.
5. Determine the approach, type, and number of interviews necessary. There are multiple approaches to interviewing applicants.

    Pre-screening interview tests may be used to learn skills, abilities, and personalities of candidates.

    One-on-One, face-to-face interview in which the manager or personnel director interviews the candidate.

    Situational interview in which the candidate is put in an actual work scenario.

    Panel or team interview in which the candidate meets with, and is interviewed by, several individuals from the organization.

6. Determine the types of questions to use during the interview.

    Hypothetical questions ask how a candidate would handle a possible situation.

    Example: Imagine that you suspect an employee is stealing money from the cash drawer. How would you handle this situation?

    Behavioral based questions ask a candidate to reveal how they have handled a situation in the past.

    Example: Tell me about a time you had to use creativity to complete a project.

    Actual or critical incident questions ask how a candidate would handle a current situation in the work place.

    Example: We are currently experiencing a twenty percent decline in our outdoor apparel line. What would you do in order to improve this decline?

7. Prepare a schedule of questions.

Résumé Questions

For this assignment you will have the opportunity to practice answers to questions you may receive about your résumé from employers. It is necessary to be prepared to fully explain what is on your résumé and this activity will help you practice these answers.

You will need to bring three copies of your résumé to class. Your résumé should include at least the following sections: Education, Experience, and Skills/Honors/Activities.

The instructor will divide the class into groups of four students and assign each person in the group a letter for identification purposes during this activity. The letters used are A, B, C, and D. Student D will give each person in the group a copy of his/her résumé to begin Round 1.

During each round, each individual in the group will take a turn asking the interviewee about a section of his/her résumé. Follow the schedule below during each round. The instructor will allow two minutes for each question and answer. If the interviewee responds to the question before the two minutes is up the interviewer must be prepared with probing questions. The instructor will notify the students when the two minutes is up so the next student can ask his/her question.

Round 1: *Student A:* Will ask a question about the Education section.
Student B: Will ask a question about the Experience section.
Student C: Will ask a question about the Skills/Honors/Activities section.
Student D: Will answer questions regarding his/her resume.

Round 2: *Student B:* Will ask a question about the Education section.
Student C: Will ask a question about the Experience section.
Student D: Will ask a question about the Skills/Honors/Activities section.
Student A: Will answer questions regarding his/her resume.

Round 3: *Student D:* Will ask a question about the Education section.
Student A: Will ask a question about the Experience section.
Student B: Will ask a question about the Skills/Honors/Activities section.
Student C: Will answer questions regarding his/her resume.

Round 4: *Student C:* Will ask a question about the Education section.
Student D: Will ask a question about the Experience section.
Student A: Will ask a question about the Skills/Honors/Activities section.
Student B: Will answer questions regarding his/her resume.

After the fourth round, another student in the group will distribute his/her résumé to the members of the group and the rounds begin over.

Recruiting Schedule

Imagine you are a recruiter for the Bremerton Fire Protection District. When you became the recruiter for this fire district, you found this list of questions used during previous interviews. These questions are not in logical order and they do not include any possible probes. The schedule also does not include any transitions. Redo this schedule by organizing the questions so it flows better; add possible secondary/probes and transitions.

Out of all the schools you could have attended, why did you choose this university?

Please tell me your strengths.

Where do you see yourself five years from now?

Tell me about a time when you had to work under pressure.

Why does a career as a firefighter appeal to you?

Tell me about your contribution to your college expenses.

What is one of your weaknesses?

What would you like to be doing 10 years from now?

How would your friends describe you?

Tell me about a time when you had to step up and take charge.

Do you like to work in teams or on your own? Why?

How has your education prepared you for this position?

Why are you the best candidate for this position?

Tell me about a time you had to use creativity to solve a problem.

What activities were you involved in at your university?

What questions do you have for me?

STAR Method

Behavioral Based Interviewing

Behavioral Based Questions	Provide an example of a time when you experienced group conflict. How did you help to resolve this conflict?	Provide an example of how you prioritize tasks between classes, homework, and your job.	Provide an example of a time when you provided leadership within a group to delegate tasks.
S **Situation** = Describe			
T What **task** was involved?			
A What **action** did you take?			
R What was the **result**? What did you learn? What will you do differently in the future?			

Preparing to Interview

As a recruiter, it is necessary for you to be familiar with the requirements of an open position as well as the characteristics, skills, talents, and education requirements. As an applicant, it is to your advantage to look at and analyze the position from the recruiter's perspective. Doing this will help you be a better applicant.

For this assignment you need to find a position announcement or job posting for a position you would like to have in your future.

Answer the following questions regarding this announcement:

1. What are the duties of this position? Which four are most important? Why?

2. What skills and talents must an individual have in order to be successful in this position?

3. What education should an individual have in order to be successful in this position?

4. What personal characteristics and attributes should an individual have in order to be successful in this position?

5. Based on your answers above, write five effective behavior based questions.

6. Imagine you are the applicant for this position. Answer the questions you developed in Number 5.

Hiring Decisions

Recruiting a new employee is an expensive venture for organizations. If the wrong employee is selected it can be disastrous. Hiring the wrong employee will set a company back several thousand dollars. Unfortunately, many hiring managers are unprepared. They have no formal training or even participated in a workshop or course on interviewing. It is necessary for recruiters to become better interviewers. Now that you have learned about Recruiting Interviews, make a list of the interview process/steps and suggestions to follow to help recruiters become more effective.

Recruiting Interview Question Practice

Below is a portion of a job description for a receptionist position. Review this description.

Qualifications

To perform this job successfully, an individual must be able to perform each essential duty satisfactorily. The essential duties include:

♦ Ability to read and interpret manuals, procedural forms, operating and maintenance instructions.

♦ Effective reading, writing, and oral communication skills, including speaking in front of groups for training purposes.

♦ Ability to manage multiple projects and deadlines simultaneously.

♦ Ability to delegate tasks and supervise two part-time office assistants.

Write questions below based on this section of the description.

Hypothetical question regarding multiple deadlines.

_____

_____

Behavior based question regarding public speaking.

_____

_____

Behavior based question regarding multitasking.

_____

_____

Critical incident question based on supervision of office assistants.

_____

_____

As the recruiter, you decide to use a situational interview. Describe how you would create this.

Recruiting Interview Questions

While interviewing possible future employees it is necessary to understand the objective of each question. Knowing the objective will help the interviewer prepare effective secondary/probing questions.

For example, if an interviewer is concerned about a candidate's ability to get along with others as well as their interpersonal skills the interviewer may ask:

Interviewer: How do you establish working relationships with new people?
Response: I easily and quickly establish positive relationships with individuals.

Knowing that the interviewer has the goal of learning about a candidate's ability to get along with others, an effective secondary/probing question might be:

Interviewer: In the past, how have you established these relationships?

For the following interview questions, write effective secondary/probing questions, keeping the objective of the question in mind.

1. Objective: Did the interviewee prepare and research effectively for this interview.

   Interviewer: What do you know about our organization?
   Possible Secondary/Probes:

   Interviewer: How did you prepare for this interview?
   Possible Secondary/Probes:

   Interviewer: What can you do for this company?
   Possible Secondary/Probes:

2. Objective: Determine whether this position, company, and career field are right for the interviewee.

    Interviewer: Will you be happy here?
    Possible Secondary/Probes:

    Interviewer: What are your goals?
    Possible Secondary/Probes:

    Interviewer: Where are you headed in life?
    Possible Secondary/Probes:

    Interviewer: Why have you chosen this particular field?
    Possible Secondary/Probes:

3. Objective: To learn how well the interviewee can articulate and present him or herself.

    Interviewer: Tell me about yourself.
    Possible Secondary/Probes:

4. Objective: To learn about the interviewee's thought process and how the interviewee solves problems.

    Interviewer: Give me an example of a problem you encountered at school or work and explain how you solved it.
    Possible Secondary/Probes:

Image © Maridav, 2012. Used under license from Shutterstock, Inc.

Employment

e x e r c i s e s

♦ Conduct a self-analysis. Later in this chapter is a Career Interest Assessment list of links to help you accomplish this. Review these and complete one of them. After having done a self-analysis and after having reviewed/read the additional articles for this chapter, come up with an answer to the question, "So, tell me about yourself." The answer to this question should be typed and turned in.

♦ Turn in a completed résumé and cover letter.

♦ Create a list of ten qualities you possess that would make you an asset to an organization. Next, go out and research what ten qualities employers are looking for.
  ◇ What did you find?
  ◇ How are your qualities similar? Different?
  ◇ What will you have to do to obtain/gain these qualities to make yourself more marketable to a corporation?

♦ Conduct research on Regis Philbin and his employment record. Write up your responses in a one page essay. What did you find? Does this impact your thought process about employment hunting?

♦ Create stories for different strengths you have (conflict management, time management, multitasking, dependability, etc.).

- Imagine that your supervisor has asked you to help select individuals to hire for "seasonal" work. Write a list of ten questions that you would like to ask the applicants.

- Get a copy of *The Washington Post, USA Today, Chicago Tribune,* etc. Find the employment section and locate a job that you find to be interesting. After you've read through the announcement, draft two lists of questions. List one would be questions that the employer would ask of potential interviewees applying for this position. List two would be questions that an interviewee would want to know about this company.

- Most recruiters are asking behavior based questions. Pretend that you are at an interview playing the role of interviewee. How would you answer the following questions:
  ◇ Tell me about a problem you've handled in the last year? How successful was your solution?
  ◇ Give me an example of a good decision you've made in the last year? Why do you think it was a good decision?
  ◇ What were the biggest obstacle(s) you had to overcome to get where you are today? How did you overcome them?
  ◇ What is the most difficult situation you have faced?
  ◇ What have you done that shows initiative?
  ◇ What are your greatest strengths? Weaknesses?

d i s c u s s i o n   q u e s t i o n s

- If you had to define the word "career" how would you do that?
- Do generations differ in their mindset of how to "work"?
- Have you ever changed your mind about the direction of your career? Why? How did this change occur? What made this change occur?
- What do you think a self-analysis could help you accomplish/realize?
- Why is it important to research a career field that you might be interested in?
- Where is a good place to start your career search? Why?
- Are career fairs beneficial to someone starting the job search?
- How do social networking sites impact your potential to get a job?
- How would you react if an applicant came to an interview in jeans and a t-shirt? How would you interpret the situation if this candidate was the best qualified and had the best interview?
- During an interview, does the interviewee also interview the interviewer? Explain.
- How important is the context of your interview? Describe.
- What types of nonverbal behavior would you expect to see during an employment interview? What types would you expect not to see used during an employment interview?
- When creating your résumé, should you include high school activities? Why or why not?
- Discuss the benefits and drawbacks of a chronological résumé? Functional? Combination?
- Have you ever "fibbed" on a résumé or application form? If so, what was it about? Did you get caught? What is the danger in lying?

- Discuss what you think your résumé should look like (in terms of appearance at first glance). Are there any items to stay away from?
- How should you respond during an interview when you are asked about your weaknesses?
- What would you do if you were asked an unlawful question during an interview?
  - ◇ Have you ever been asked an unlawful question?
  - ◇ How did you respond?
- At the end of an interview, what might be some questions you could ask an interviewer?
- Discuss the importance of small talk during an Employment Interview. Are there things you should stay away from discussing?
- Is it a good/bad thing to pause before answering a question during an Employment Interview?

Developing Your 60-Second Commercial

Mandy Nycz
Assistant Director of Career Services
St. Norbert College, Wisconsin

Tell me about yourself. If you have ever been on a job interview you have probably been asked this dreaded question. Many interviewers start with this question because they can get an overall sense of who you are in a very short time. You want to make sure you give a positive first impression when answering this question as it can set the tone for the entire interview.

"Tell me about yourself" can be a challenging question for multiple reasons. First, it is very ambiguous, and most people are unsure of the type of information the interviewer wants to hear. Second, the interviewee is typically uncertain how long the answer should be. One of the biggest mistakes interviewees make is talking too long or failing to wrap up their answers in a succinct manner.

Interviewers ask this question to get an overall sense about you, but they are not interested in hearing a 15-minute recitation of your life story. Rather, they are interested in a brief overview of your career-related background, which is why the 60-second commercial is the best strategy to use when faced with this vague question. You will be able to structure and deliver your answer in a clear and concise manner. Not only can you use this strategy in response to "tell me about yourself," but also to introduce yourself at education career fairs, to network at professional events, or even to mingle at a party.

The key to an effective 60-second commercial is to keep it career-related. This strategy should be focused on you, and should highlight your education, experience, and goals. Your 60-second commercial can be easily organized by answering the three following questions.

Who Are You and Where Are You Now?

Your answer should focus specifically on your college education. Don't include your high school education. Include the following information:

- The college or university from which you have or will graduate
- Location: city and state, especially if you attended a lesser known school or are applying for positions out of state
- Graduation date: include the month and year of your graduation
- Degree
- Major/Minor: include all majors and minors
- Emphasis or concentration areas
- Teaching certification.

Where Have You Been?

You should focus specifically on your experiences, particularly your career-related experiences, as these will be most relevant to the employer. When describing your experience, do not just state where you completed your student teaching. Rather, be sure to include specific skills that are transferable to the position for which you are interviewing and make sure the skills are relevant to the employer. A good way to ensure that you are discussing the proper skills is to familiarize yourself with the job description. That job description will include a list of requirements which will help you tailor your response to show that your skills and experience meet or exceed the requirements. Possible topics to include:

- student teaching experience
- career-related experience
- additional work experience
- volunteer experience
- study or teaching abroad experience
- leadership experience (college only)
- activities (college only).

Where Are You Going?

Your answer should focus on your career objective or future goals and the ways in which you can be of assistance to the school or district with which you are interviewing. Make sure you do your homework before the interview and complete adequate research on the position, school, and district so you can specifically address the needs of that particular school or district. You will want to explain how your unique skill set meets their needs.

Final Thoughts

The best way to prepare your 60-second commercial is to first write a rough draft response to the three questions above. Next—practice, practice, practice! Say the words out loud so that you are accustomed to hearing yourself talk about your skills and experience. You do not want to sound like you have memorized your response. Rather, you should practice until you sound natural when discussing yourself and your skills. By taking the time to prepare well your unique 60-second commercial, you will ensure that when the time comes to answer the "tell me about yourself" question, you will be able to respond in a clear, concise, and most importantly, confident manner.

60-Second Commercial Example

I am currently a senior at St. Norbert College in De Pere, Wisconsin. I will graduate this May with a bachelor of arts degree in elementary education, a minor in early childhood education, and certification in early childhood/middle childhood.

During my student teaching experience at Westwood Elementary School, I managed a diverse classroom of 23 third grade students and designed and implemented lesson plans for all curriculum areas. I chose to take advantage of the opportunity to complete a portion of my student teaching in Ireland, which helped to develop my sensitivity to other cultural values and customs and exposed me to a different educational system. I quickly learned to adapt to new and challenging situations.

In addition to my student teaching, I interacted with children in learning activities and playtime on a daily basis as a part-time assistant pre-school teacher at the college's children's center.

I was a member of the varsity track and field team for four years, and during my last two years, I was selected by teammates and coaches to serve as captain. This experience taught me to handle multiple responsibilities while successfully managing academics and athletics.

I am seeking a 3rd grade teaching position at Heritage Elementary School. I will bring to this position my passion for education, my experience student teaching both here and abroad, as well as strong leadership skills and an interest in coaching athletics.

There's a New Game in Town: Successful Interviewing in the Electronic Age

Jody Shelton, Executive Director
American Association of School Personnel Administrators, Kansas

Over the past 20 years, interviewing has changed tremendously with the rapid increase in use of e-mail, electronic job applications, and online interviews. Despite the change in format of communications, however, it's important to remember that many of the basic interviewing rules of yesterday still apply in today's fast-paced, electronic world.

With preparation and attention to detail, you can increase your chances for a successful interview. Here are a few basic rules that still apply in today's new interviewing environment.

The First Impression Counts

You can only make a first impression once, and first impressions count when trying to get the teaching job of your dreams. The first impression comes with the first contact you have with the school district, whether that's when the district receives your application electronically or by mail, when you contact the human relations office to inquire about the application process, or at a campus recruitment or screening interview.

If your first encounter is direct contact, put your best foot forward in dress and manner. If it is the application or résumé, proofread, proofread, proofread. Even small typos can contribute to your application being passed over.

This is especially important to remember in online and e-mail interaction which is often interpreted as a more casual form of communicating. Spend as much time proofreading your e-mail communications as you would a formal letter printed on paper. You might even print out and read your e-mail draft to double-check for typos before you hit the "send" button. Make sure you attach requested documents and that they, too, have been proofread.

Body Language Speaks Louder than Words

Body language, or nonverbal communication, is easily forgotten in a world where the majority of communication takes place over the phone or the Internet, yet it is a powerful detail to consider. In an interview, as much as 90 percent of the impression you make comes from your body language. This includes your handshake, posture, eye contact, and body movements.

Give a firm handshake when appropriate to create a positive impression regarding your level of confidence. If you are sitting during the interview, be sure you sit up and a little forward in your chair with a slight bend toward the interviewer. This shows the interest you have in the position.

Make direct eye contact before, during, and at the close of the interview, promoting a feeling of confidence and interest. Holding eye contact for at least four seconds is a good measure. You should also think about your body movements. Maintain a calm and in control feeling by keeping body movements to a minimum. Crossing and uncrossing your legs, continually blinking your eyes, or even clasping and unclasping your hands can be interpreted as a lack of confidence.

Listen to Questions

Take time to listen to each question. After we have heard just the first few words of a question, we tend to begin trying to think about what our answer is going to be. Instead, take time first to really listen to the question. Be sure you are going down the right path with your answer by keying in to the entire question. This is equally important when you participate in online screening interviews. Take time to read and interpret each question carefully before answering and moving on to the next question.

Treat the Human Resources Office Team as Your Best Friend

Your interview begins the moment you have some kind of contact with the human resources office. Whether that contact is by e-mail, phone, or in person, you need to treat your contact as you would treat your best friend.

If your first encounter is on the phone, be friendly and pleasant. The first person who contacts you regarding an application or interview often has been instructed to conduct a mini-screening interview when he or she communicates with you. Make that person feel the smile you have on your face. If the contact is in an office, be sure you start that encounter with a sincere, friendly smile. Office staffs are powerful team members, and you should be sure to give them your best in any contact you have with them.

Follow Up After the Interview

Many people forget one of the most important steps of the interview process: following up after the interview. While sending an e-mail thank you note seems convenient and is sometimes sufficient, it can make a much stronger impression to send a handwritten note on a thank-you card. Besides showing your initiative and genuine interest in the job, it gives you a chance to have your name in front of the interviewer again.

While electronic communication has made many of our jobs and lives easier, the quick and automated routes to applying and interviewing for a job are not excuses to disregard the details of professionalism and personal touch. Effective communications—electronic, written, verbal, and nonverbal—are all still essential in demonstrating that you are a prepared and worthy candidate.

The Telephone Interview: Your New Job Is Calling

Julia Overton-Healy, Director for Career Development Mansfield University of Pennsylvania

Administrators who need to find qualified candidates while containing recruitment costs have taken a cue from the business world by using telephone interviews. Candidates, too, are opting for a telephone conversation before committing themselves to the rigors or expenses of traveling to a site visit. Telephone interviews have advantages and disadvantages.

- Advantages: allows the interviewer to screen potential candidates, cuts down on recruitment costs, and is time efficient.
- Disadvantage: doesn't allow either participant to observe nonverbal cues, such as facial expressions, gestures, or eye contact.

Phone interviewers are essentially looking for specific things: how well you communicate verbally, how closely your qualifications and experience match their needs, and your willingness to relocate.

12 Tips for Top-Notch Telephone Interviewing

- *Prepare yourself as if this were a face-to-face interview.* Dress in business attire; anticipate questions you will be asked; frame your responses; and prepare a list of questions you need to have answered.
- *Have your documentation in front of you.* Have right at hand the job announcement, as well as your cover letter, résumé, transcripts, and letters of recommendation.
- *Schedule the appointment for a time when you won't feel pressured or be distracted.* Plan for 10 minutes before the call to calm yourself and 15 minutes after the call to summarize and clarify any notes you made.
- *Try to take the call in a room that has no distraction.* Turn off the television and radio, face a blank wall, or do anything that will help you concentrate.
- *Take notes.* During the conversation jot down the questions your interviewer asks and any information he or she offers (e.g., class load, extracurricular obligations, etc.).
- *Try to offer concrete and vivid examples.* As you answer questions, examples will help demonstrate what you have done, and they also help express your personality.
- *If you need time to think, say so.* Five seconds of dead air in person doesn't feel very long, but on the phone, it's an eternity. Rephrasing the question is one way to buy time, and it also helps you clarify exactly what is being asked.
- *Be concise.* Long, rambling responses will seem even more so on the phone. Stay on topic and answer the question.

◆ *Listen carefully to how your interviewer responds to what you say.* If you have a sense that your answer was not understood, ask if you need to rephrase your thoughts.

◆ *Stand up.* The tone of your voice is the result of complex systems within your body and you'll sound more professional and mature if you stand up.

◆ *Don't eat, drink, chew gum, or smoke.* The noise will be heard.

◆ *Smile!* Your voice tone changes when you smile, and even if you cannot be seen, your enthusiasm will be felt.

Bonus tip: Before your interviewer hangs up (let him or her hang up first!), find out what the next steps are in the process. Then you'll know what to expect and the uncertainty won't drive you nuts!

Behavior Based Questions

- What is the most difficult situation you have had to face thus far in your life?
- Provide an example of something that you have done which shows initiative?
- What do you feel were (or are) your most significant accomplishment(s) in your academic career?
- Tell us about one of the most difficult/demanding tasks, at either work or school that you've had to handle. How did you handle that? What was the outcome?
- Provide an example of a time when you found a mistake in a project/paper you were working on. How did you notice these mistakes? What did you do to fix them?
- When working in small groups, often times there can be conflict. Think of strategies you've used in a small group when there were large differences of opinion. How did you solve these problems of difference?
- Give another example of a time when you worked with a group/team. What were your goals? What difficulties did the group have? What was your role in this group?
- Describe what you consider to be the most creative thing that you have done in your work experiences thus far.
- We all have some disappointments, especially during our academic journeys. What was a disappointment you had? How did you pick yourself up after this experience?
- Describe a problem you've handled in the last year? How did you handle this problem? Was it a good decision?
- Provide an example of a good decision you've made in the last year. Why do you think it was a good decision?
- What were the biggest obstacle(s) you had to overcome to get where you are today? How did you overcome them?
- Tell me about a time when you've felt pressured. How did you deal with it? What happened?
- Tell me about a time you were frustrated at work. How did you handle the frustration?
- Of the jobs you've had in the last two years, what has been the biggest problem you've faced and how did you handle it?
- Think of a good or bad work experience you've had in the past. What was it? What did you do? What did you learn from it?
- Describe a situation when you had to adjust because priorities were changed.
- Describe a work situation when you interacted with individuals who were from culturally diverse backgrounds (could also be socially or economically diverse as well). Were you successful? If yes, how? If not, why?

Practice answering each of these questions using the STAR Method!

Who Else Has Your Traits?

In order to help you discover your strengths, we are going to complete an activity.

- First, list your strengths/traits on paper. Narrow down the list to the top three that represent you.
  - ◇ Make sure your three traits are not the same in meaning (similar).
    - Example: people person, friendly, outgoing
    - Example: hardworking, loyal, dependable
    - Example: likeable, people person, good communicator.
- Second, introduce yourself to your classmates and reveal your three strengths to each of them. They will in turn list their strengths to you. Pay attention—listen.

Now that you've learned everyone's strengths, write a reaction paper including a discussion of the following items:

- What did you hear most often (overused)—do you think you will make a memorable impression with your strength if the employer heard the same words from all the candidates?
- What was memorable (unusual)? (For instance: problem solver, analytical, inquisitive, conflict manager, negotiator, etc.)
- How can you change your traits to make yourself stand out? (Remember, a recruiter/interviewer probably hears the same things that you heard in this activity.)
- Now, think of a specific position you want. How are your skills needed in the profession?
- Which of these skills/traits are most compatible with the job that you want?

Career Interest Assessment Helps

- Illinois Career Information Systems: http://ilcis.intocareers.org
  Click on Assessments and Links at the bottom left of the home page.

- Michigan Reach Out website: http://www.reachoutmichigan.org/career/nextstop/car_plan.html

- Quintessential Career Resources: http://www.quintcareers.com/career_resources.html
  Includes articles, advice, and tests/quizzes for your job search/preparation.

- MAPP assessment where you can identify your ideal career and more:
  http://www.assessment.com/MAPPMembers/Welcome.asp?accnum=06-5669-000.00

- Career and Personality Tests http://jobsearch.about.com/od/careertests/a/careertests.htm

- A free career assessment test: www.careerkey.com

- Culturefit allows you to determine the ideal organizational culture for you:
  www.careerleader.com/sstn/culture-test.html

- Keirsey Temperament Sorter personality test: http://www.keirsey.com/

- A site which contains general occupational information. A "skill" test lets you select skills you
  possess and match them to occupations: http://online.onetcenter.org/

Make sure to visit your local University Counseling Center, Advising Office, or Career Service Center.
Many of them have a variety of assessment tests.

Mock International Interview

For this activity, you will have the opportunity to put into practice everything you have learned about interviewing in another culture. Each group will participate in a panel interview. The group will play the role of interviewer for the culture they have researched and presented information about.

The classroom will be organized into stations and each station will represent a different culture. Your instructor will choose which day each culture will play the role of interviewer. All other students will play the role of interviewee on that day. Interviewees will rotate to each station and participate in a mock Employment Interview in that culture. You will be expected to act out the traditions and customs of the culture being represented. For example, if it is customary to offer guests a cup of tea, make sure and do this (your instructor may provide any props needed for this interview). Interviewees should know from the group presentations how to act and interact with the members of the culture being represented.

Interviewers will evaluate each interviewee as they are being interviewed.

During this mock interview, you will be able to participate as an interviewer and interviewee. To fully understand the concept of interviewing, you and your classmates will also act as interviewer. You should live up to the role of interviewee and interviewer in a realistic manner. Pay special attention to the following.

Appropriate delivery for the culture (nonverbal behavior, energetic, dynamic):

a. Body language—posture, natural gestures, level of interest, level of relaxation.
b. Appropriate eye contact
c. Vocal qualities—effective rate, energy, volume, articulation, clear speaking style (free of jargon, slang, and grammatical errors).

Appearance:

a. Professional dress (hats off, no low cut tops, no jeans, shirts tucked in, no gum)
b. Mannerisms

As the interviewer you will prepare a moderate schedule so that you can ask the interviewee relevant questions.

The feedback on the evaluation forms should be thoughtful and will be graded based on the thoroughness and quality of feedback.

Interviewing Book Report

You will choose a book of your interest that relates to the topic of interviewing. There is a suggested list of books below. Please select a recent book (published 2005 or later).

Book Selection

Your book must be approved by your instructor. Turn in your book selection by _____.

The number of people reading the same book will be limited to two, so if your first choice is a very popular one, you may have to choose another. You have a better chance of acceptance of your first choice if your selection is made early.

Book Report and Presentation

You will prepare a typed book report or outline of the book and give an oral presentation to the class.

The book report needs to be three to four pages double spaced. If you choose to prepare an outline, it should be three to four pages. Please prepare a full sentence outline so another reader can understand the book from your outline.

Include the following in your report/outline:

- What did you learn about the interviewing process from this book?
- How will this book benefit you during the interview process?
- Would you recommend this book to your classmates or friend?
- Don't try to summarize the whole book—you will not have enough room or time.
- Give an overview of what the book is about, then pick a few issues to discuss.
- Think about your classmates and what would benefit them, then include this in your report.
- Writing mechanics (grammar, spelling, punctuation, etc.) will count for some of the grade.

The campus library may have some books, but in almost all cases, only one copy, and it could be checked out. You may be able to get some books from Interlibrary Loan, which may take a week or more (and you may have to return them after only a week or two). Some of the books are available in local libraries or bookstores. Start early.

Possible Book Report Selections

- *How Would You Move Mt. Fuji? Microsoft's Cult of the Puzzle* by William Poundstone
- *More Best Answers to the 201 Most Frequently Asked Interview Questions* by Matthew J. DeLuca and Nanette F. DeLuca
- *201 Best Questions to Ask on Your Interview* by John Kador
- *Knock 'Em Dead* by Martin Yate
- *101 Great Answers to the Toughest Interview Questions* by Ron Fry
- *High Impact Hiring: How to Interview and Select Outstanding Employees* by Del J. Still
- *Behavior Based Interviewing: Selecting the Right Person for the Job* by Terry L. Fitzwater

- *Hire With Your Head: Using POWER Hiring to Build Great Teams* by Lou Adler
- *The Talent Edge: A Behavioral Approach to Hiring, Developing, and Keeping Top Performers* by David S. Cohen
- *Topgrading: How Leading Companies Win by Hiring, Coaching, and Keeping the Best People* by Bradford D. Smart
- *Get the Interview Every Time: Fortune 500 Hiring Professional's Tips for Writing Winning Résumés and Cover Letters* by Brenda Greene
- *The 250 Job Interview Questions: You'll Most Likely Be Asked . . . and the Answers That Will Get You Hired!* by Peter Veruki
- *The Resume Handbook: How to Write Outstanding Resumes and Cover Letters for Every Situation* by Arthur Rosenberg and David V. Hizer
- *The Career Change Resume: How to Reinvent Your Resume and Land Your Dream Job* by Kim Isaacs and Karen Hofferber
- *e-Resumes: Everything You Need to Know About Using Electronic Resumes to Tap into Today's Hot Job Market* by Susan Britton Whitcomb and Pat Kendall
- *Cover Letters That Knock 'Em Dead* (Knock 'em Dead Series) by Martin Yate

International Business Assignment

For this assignment, you and three classmates (working as a group) will choose a country and research the dominant culture in that country and present your findings in a class presentation. First, choose a country from the following list:

Singapore	Australia	China
Spain	Japan	Canada
Belize	Mexico	Saudi Arabia
Brazil	Russia	Morocco

Your group will conduct research on this culture and share what you learn in a classroom presentation. Your research and presentation must center on international etiquette, specifically how it relates to interviewing. In the future, you and/or some of your classmates may work abroad or work for a company that is on United States soil but owned by citizens of another country and conducts business according to the customs of their home culture. You must know how to communicate verbally and nonverbally with others from a diverse background in the business and corporate world. You must also be knowledgeable about customs and traditions so you do not offend or embarrass yourself or the interviewer.

Some of the areas suggested for research include:

- Body language
- Proper dining etiquette
- Cooperation
- Approach to time
- Competition
- Gender differences
- Laws different from U.S. laws
- Materialism
- Dependence
- Appearance/dress

This is not an exhaustive list. There are numerous other topics and areas to help you learn the customs and traditions that guide behavior in a culture.

Presentation: Your group will present information about your country/culture to the class in a 20-minute presentation. All members of your group must participate equally in this presentation.

Grading: Your group will be graded on the quality and credibility of your research, how appropriate and applicable the information is to your interviewing class, and your presentation skills.

International Etiquette

There are entire books devoted to the subject of international etiquette. Many public libraries and bookstores carry these books. Try looking under the following subjects: International Etiquette, Travel Etiquette, and Business Etiquette. Some of these books discuss the rules for many countries, and others focus on a particular country.

There are also numerous websites devoted to international etiquette. Some are listed below:

- International Business Center: http://www.internationalbusinesscenter.org/
- Cultural etiquette around the world:
  http://www.ediplomat.com/np/cultural_etiquette/cultural_etiquette.htm
- International Business Etiquette, Manners, & Culture: http://www.cyborlink.com/
- Doing Business in Foreign Countries by LexisNexis:
  http://law.lexisnexis.com/infopro/zimmermans/disp.aspx?z=14010
- Global Road Warrior: http://www.globalroadwarrior.com/index.asp

Do not overlook international students, instructors, and those who have lived in the country you are researching.

Career Vision Paper

Much research indicates that a common trait of successful people is that they have a clear idea of where they want to go; indeed, they have a vision of what they want their lives to look like. Unfortunately, most of us don't take the time to put that vision together. Many people spend more time planning a party than they do planning their life. This project is designed to give you the opportunity to build your professional future at least in your mind's eye.

Do some serious thinking about your professional future before you write a single word for this project. If you are struggling to determine a vision or goal for your professional life you may want to try one of the following activities before you begin writing your paper.

a. Conduct a self-assessment. See the self-assessment resources in your workbook.
b. Write a few paragraphs outlining what you want your life to look like two years from now, five years from now, and ten years from now.
c. Write your own obituary. Imagine you are 100 years old and have lived a full life. List your employment positions, careers, and professional awards and accomplishments.
d. Pretend that tomorrow morning when you wake up you have your dream career. Write about this career. Where do you work, who do you work with, what type of work do you do, etc.?

Once you have determined your future professional goal write about it. This should be double spaced, 12 point font and four pages. Include a detailed description of the professional position you want to have in ten years. You will, at the very least, describe the sector or area in which you desire a career, the geographic location, the size of the organization, and your position (detail here is important).

Also answer the following questions:

♦ What do you anticipate the best things to be about the position?
♦ What training and experiences are essential for entering this field/position?
♦ What do you anticipate will be the challenges or problems in the position?
♦ What has to happen for you to achieve this desired future?
♦ What are you doing right now to make this a reality?
♦ What else could you be doing to "stack the deck" for yourself for this career future?
♦ Are you now doing these things? If not, why aren't you doing these things?

Research will be necessary in order to intelligently answer some of the questions. There are numerous published resources, experts in the field, and various sources to help you in your research. Try some of the following resources:

Department of Labor Bureau of Labor Statistics webpage (http://www.bls.gov/)

United States Bureau of Labor (http://www.dol.gov/)

The Riley Guide (http://www.rileyguide.com/)

Career Resources, Career Guide, Online Education and Degree Directory (http://www.careers.org)

The Career Services Office at your school

Type a three page paper explaining your career vision. Include a bibliography for your sources.

Networking Activity

The goal of this assignment is to network with three individuals you do not know and learn as much as you can about a topic of your choice. You will use your own circle of friends and acquaintances to network with these people. Over 60% of positions are filled through networking, so learning to network effectively is to your advantage. This activity will give you practice networking.

Directions:

1. List topics that you would like to know more about. On your list you may include a hobby, vacation, sport, town, or an aspect of your future career. Choose one of these topics.
2. Talk to your immediate circle of friends and acquaintances and tell them you are looking for someone who can provide information about your topic. Get the name, address, phone number, etc. of the person your friend/acquaintance refers you to. Your friend is NOT the person you network with. The person you network with needs to be someone outside of your immediate circle of friends/acquaintances. It should be someone you do not know.
3. After you have obtained the contact information from your friend, contact the person you want to network with. When you contact this person you will need to introduce yourself and explain the reason for your contact. One suggestion for this is:

"Hello, my name is _____ and our mutual friend ____(name of friend)____ gave me your contact information. He said you might be able to provide some information about _____(name your topic)_____ . I would like to talk to someone like you, who is knowledgeable about this topic. Do you have time to meet with me for about 20 minutes to talk?"

Do meet this person in a public place (library, University Union, residence hall lounge, etc.).

4. You will need to prepare a list of questions that you want to ask before you meet with this person. Learn as much as you can from this person about your topic.
5. While you are meeting with this person take notes about what you learn (be sure to ask for permission first). Note taking is something very difficult to master as an interviewer. The best way to improve your note taking abilities is to practice. Try using key words while taking notes rather than writing full sentences.
6. Complete this networking activity by _____.
   Come to class prepared to discuss this activity with your classmates.

Networking as a Get to Know Your Classmates Activity

More than half of all positions are filled through networking. Most people know someone who landed a job through networking. This activity will allow you to practice networking with your classmates.

1. With your classmates, form two circles, one interior and one exterior. Have the interior circle face the exterior circle. Make sure everyone has a partner. There can be a group of three if there is an odd number of students present.
2. Introduce yourself to each other, tell where you are from, your major, etc. and then talk about the career you would like to enter.
3. Other students in the class may know someone in the field and can give the name of a contact to you.
4. Switch partners after three minutes by having the students in the outer circle move one person to the right.
5. Each time you meet a new student work on perfecting your introduction and explanation of your desired career.
6. After practicing this numerous times in class, you are now ready to network with others outside of the classroom setting.

Networking Tree

Use the following networking form to begin your networking contact list.

List the following: Friends, acquaintances (hair dresser, mechanic, etc.), relatives and family members, family connections, former employers, alumni, internship directors, professors and teachers, academic advisor, financial aid advisor.

Add addresses, phone numbers, email addresses, etc. to all on your network tree.

As you network with each individual record what you learned from them.

Make sure you send a thank you note to those who help you.

Networking Contact List

Contact	Title	Place of Business	Address	City/State/Zip	Work Phone	Personal Phone	E-Mail	Info./Notes	Date of Last Contact

Your Life Stories

As you know, during Employment Interviews recruiters often ask a lot of behavioral based questions. One way to answer these questions is to provide a story in the answer that can truly highlight your skills (and the traits that they seek). By providing various types of stories (using the STAR Method), you'll be able to competently answer the questions while providing examples of your life experiences. So, create stories based on the following concepts from your real life experiences thus far.

Dealing with conflict

Handling stress

Difficult co-worker

Outstanding customer service

Leadership skills

10

Appraisal/Performance

exercises

- During your annual Appraisal/Performance Interview, your supervisor gave you the chance to write down some thoughts (self-analysis) of your performance over the last year. What would you want to make sure this narrative included?

- Pretend that you are an employer preparing for an Appraisal/Performance Interview. How would you go about preparing? What type of materials would you need?

- Collect three to five appraisal/performance interview documents (blank) from three to five companies.
  - ◇ What similarities do you notice?
  - ◇ What are the differences?

- Set up a time to speak with someone who does appraisal/performance interviews on your campus. When talking with this individual, find out about their Appraisal/Performance Interview process. Be sure to include (in your interview) some of the following questions:
  - ◇ Which model/type of Appraisal/Performance Interview is used in this office?
    - Is it effective?
  - ◇ How many individuals are involved in the Appraisal/Performance Interview process?
  - ◇ Are you responsible for all the Appraisal/Performance Interviews or do you train others to do them as well?
    - If you do train, what is your process like?

◇ Do you feel that bias is ever a problem in interviews? Why or why not?

◇ If you had to group the three largest areas for improvement at your organization based on appraisal/performance interviews, what would they be?

d i s c u s s i o n   q u e s t i o n s

♦ What do you think are the true functions of an Appraisal/Performance Interview?

♦ Do you think that employees are wary of Appraisal/Performance Interviews? Why or why not?
  ◇ How can this mentality be changed?

♦ How can the climate of an Appraisal/Performance Interview be positive rather than negative?
  ◇ What factors contribute to the overall climate of this interview?

♦ Discuss how you would react to your company laying off several hundred workers through an email.

♦ If you were a supervisor at a not-for-profit company and one of your volunteers (which is how most of your organizational tasks are completed) was acting out of line, how could knowing the skills of an Appraisal/Performance Interview help in this situation?

♦ Have you ever been part of an appraisal/performance interview that had a problem arise (problem between interview and interviewee)? Did a confrontation occur? What was the outcome?

♦ How can goal setting be effective during an Appraisal/Performance Interview?

♦ How can you, the employee, help put yourself in a good position when it comes time for your Appraisal/Performance Interview?

♦ What would be some reasons why a person would receive a negative appraisal/performance evaluation?

♦ Do Appraisal/Performance Interviews build character? Why or why not?

♦ What would you do if you were just given a very unfair and negative Appraisal/Performance Interview?

♦ Have you ever been stereotyped during an Appraisal/Performance Interview? If so, what happened? How did you respond?

♦ What are the pros and cons of using a team appraisal method for Appraisal/Performance Interviews?

♦ Think of your last performance evaluation. Did you feel motivated after the appraisal? Did you feel valued by the company/organization/interviewer? How did you contribute to the interview? Did you set goals at the interview with your supervisor? Imagine you are the supervisor. What would you do differently at the next performance interview?

Anna's Performance

Below you will find an essay appraising the performance of Anna, a department manager in a large home improvement store. This appraisal was prepared by her supervisor. Read through this appraisal and then, based on what you have learned about performance appraisals (including goal setting, providing specific feedback and description, evaluating work performance, etc.) evaluate how well the supervisor appraised Anna's performance.

ANNA JONES, PERFORMANCE EVALUATION APPRAISAL, June 13, 2012

Anna is a really great person. She gets along well with the other department managers and they can rely on her to help them out when needed. Just last Friday, June 10, 2012, when the manager in housewares had to be gone, Anna stepped in and covered both departments and did an outstanding job.

I have received numerous calls from customers who have high praise for the merchandise displays in her department. The customers state that it is easy to find the needed item and the selection is excellent.

The team members under Anna's direction all gave her a good yearly evaluation. Several of her subordinates stated that Anna is a very good listener and always provides fair and sound advice and direction.

However, at times Anna does seem distracted and distant. The fixtures and displays in her department get broken easily because of the way they are handled while in her possession.

There is always lots of room for improvement. I would like Anna to focus on the suggested areas between now and next month. I will meet with Anna in 30 days to see how she is progressing.

Performance Evaluation

Your friend has just been hired as an assistant manager for Smith Pharmacy and Health, a large chain of stores in the southwest. He must supervise the hourly employees in the local store. He knows you have just learned about Appraisal/Performance Interviews in your interviewing class. Create a list of recommendations for your friend on how to prepare and conduct Appraisal/Performance Interviews. Don't forget suggestions on listening, nonverbal and verbal behaviors, opening and closing of the interview, models and approaches to consider, goal setting, and handling conflict during the interview.

Performance Resolution Scenario

Following is a text from a Performance Interview. The interviewer has called the interviewee into her office in order to try and solve a problem at work. Read this text and list what you believe went wrong with this interview (be specific). If you were the interviewer, what would you do and say differently? If you were the interviewee, what would you say and do differently?

Interviewer: Hello, Tom, please come in. Have a seat (motions to chairs across from desk).

Interviewee: Thanks (takes a seat across the desk from interviewer).

Interviewer: We are here to talk about the incident that occurred last Friday.

Interviewee: Right. There were two people involved in this incident. Why am I the only one being called into your office? Where is Jill?

Interviewer: The other person involved in this incident will be called in individually. That is procedure for incidents like this.

Interviewee: Have you talked to Jill yet?

Interviewer: That is not important for this discussion. It seems that you expect you should be able to use anger to solve problems with your coworkers.

Interviewee: That is not true.

Interviewer: I would like you to attend anger management classes through our Employee Assistance Program.

Interviewee: So, I cannot discuss my thoughts and feelings in situations with my coworkers when I do not agree?

Interviewer: Yes, in an . . .

Interviewee: (Interrupting) That is all I was doing. I just expressed my thoughts and feelings.

Interviewer: You did not do it appropriately.

Interviewee: How do you know? You were not there. You are taking the word of another employee. What if I told you Jill acted inappropriately? Would you make her attend anger management classes?

Interviewer: This meeting is about you and your behavior, not Jill's.

Interviewee: This is totally unfair.

Interviewer: Let's table this conversation until later.

Performance Interview

Following is a scenario for a Performance Interview. Answer the following questions based on what you have learned about Performance Interviews.

Jenna is the owner and manager of Uptown Tanning Salon. She has one full-time employee and two part-time employees. It is time for Jenna to conduct a performance interview for one of her part-time employees named Rachel. Rachel has been employed at the Salon for two years and has received excellent ratings in the past on her performance interviews. She is very dependable and can be counted on to fill in when the other part-time employee or the full-time employee must be out of the office. Rachel is very friendly and is well liked by the customers. She also is extremely diligent about cleaning the tanning beds and maintaining the salon according to health code. However, for the last month her performance has been slipping. Rachel seems distracted and seems to be having difficulty focusing. She has forgotten to clean the tanning beds and she has been late to work three times during the last 2 weeks. Rachel obviously needs some coaching regarding her performance. Jenna must determine how to approach this Performance Interview so that she can help Rachel improve.

1. How should Jenna open the interview with Rachel? Be specific.

2. What praise should Jenna provide to Rachel?

3. What new goals should Jenna encourage Rachel to set?

11 Helping

Image © zphoto, 2012. Used under license from Shutterstock, Inc.

e x e r c i s e s

- If you had to create a slogan for those conducting this type of interview, what would it be and why?
- Make a list of the various types of Helping Interviews that exist.
  - ◊ Go visit three "helpers" from your list and compare and contrast how they are different.

- Imagine that you work for the local hotline. How could you create an opening for the following call that you might one day receive:
  ◇ Caller 1—a student who has a friend that is abusing prescription drugs on campus.
  ◇ Caller 2—Someone who begins the conversation by stating, "I don't have anything to live for anymore because my boyfriend just broke up with me."
  ◇ Caller 3—A student who needs someone to talk to because they are having trouble getting up for classes in the morning and in general just feel "down."
- Think about the last time you went to the doctor. Make a list of the questions that you remember being asked. Now, create a list of questions that you wish you had been asked. Provide some solutions for how you could have bridged this gap.
- Watch an episode of The Doctors or Dr. Phil and answer the following questions in a one page response.
  ◇ Do you consider this to be a Helping Interview? Why or why not?
    • Do members of society consider this to be a Helping Interview?
    • Do you think society may substitute The Doctors or Dr. Phil for the "real" experience of visiting someone in the Helping profession?
      ○ Is there a danger to this?
  ◇ What type of Helping Interview would you classify this as?
  ◇ Compare what occurs on this program to the characteristics of this particular type of Helping Interview. Are they congruent?
    • If not, what is missing?
- Visit the local Counseling Center. Talk with one of the counselors about what they experience on a daily basis. Ask them about the following:
  ◇ What kind of training did he/she receive?
  ◇ How does he/she create a constructive climate for communication?
  ◇ What types of problems do they see the most of?
  ◇ What is the most difficult part about this job?
  ◇ How do they formulate questions given that they could be seeing someone new every hour of the day?
  ◇ What do they think is important about this type of interview?

discussion questions

- When is a Helping Interview most likely to occur?
- How often do you participate in a Helping Interview?
  ◇ Describe the last time you participated in one.
  ◇ What made it a Helping Interview?
  ◇ How did you respond to the situation?
- What are some of the varying philosophies in regard to Helping Interviews? Which do you feel are the most common? Why?
- How important is the setting to a Helping Interview? Why?

- Describe how seating arrangements in a Helping Interview would either add to or distract from the exchange of information?

- Are there any dangers in trying to help others? What would some of those be?

- How is trust built during a Helping Interview? What are some ways that you could build trust with another?

- How do factors (such as culture, gender, etc.) affect an interviewee's self-disclosure during a Helping Interview?
  - ◇ How can you build trust with someone of a different culture, gender, etc. during a Helping Interview?

- What types of approaches might be useful for engaging in Helping Interviews?

- How important are probes during a Helping Interview?

- Is there a correct way to help someone?

- What are some barriers to having a successful Helping Interview? For each barrier, list a possible way to overcome.

- Are Helping Interviews related to Maslow's Hierarchy of Needs? If yes, how?

Helping Interview Scenarios

With two other students, write a conversation sequence between the interviewer and interviewee for one of the following scenarios. Include at least 25 interchanges between the parties. Include effective and ineffective methods, approaches, listening, nonverbals, etc.

Develop a skit for this scenario and act out this skit to the class.

After each skit, have the class discuss what was effective for this interview, what was ineffective, and how could this interview be improved.

Scenario 1

A counselor discussing treatment options for a patient suffering from depression.

Scenario 2

A nurse practitioner answering questions from a mother prior to giving her infant scheduled immunizations.

Scenario 3

An employer trying to encourage an employee to attend anger management classes.

Scenario 4

A doctor listening to a patient explain his symptoms.

Scenario 5

A psychologist completing a patient history intake sheet with a new patient.

Helping Another

Your neighbor and friend confides in you that she has been missing several of her classes lately, sleeping more, suffering from a lack of appetite, and feeling extremely sad. Although your friend does not ask you to help her you are concerned and fear she may be suffering from depression and needs help. Write a one page response answering the following questions.

What type of listening would you use in this situation?

How would you respond to your friend?

What would you do if she reveals suicide attempts but asks you to keep her confidence?

What advice do you give her, if any at all?

Make sure you utilize what you have learned about Helping Interviews from your text and class.

Image © Kheng Guan Toh, 2012. Used under license from Shutterstock, Inc.

Persuasion

e x e r c i s e s

- Set up a meeting with your football or basketball recruiting coaches. Talk to them about how they persuade students to attend your university. What do they say? What do they use?

- Imagine that you are interviewing for a sales position. The interviewer says to you, "sell me my pen." How do you respond?

- Ask if you can talk with your college financial representative. This individual talks with potential donors to the college.
  - ◇ During your interview with this person, find out how they prepare to speak with potential donors.
  - ◇ What strategies do they use?

◇ How do they select the time and place for the meeting? Is the meeting in person or over the phone?

◇ How do they show flexibility to the donors?

◇ What typical way do they use to close the interview?

◆ In the United States right now, one of the "hot" topics is Gay Marriage and Civil Union amendments. You are a student wanting to get more information on this topic for your upcoming debate class. Your side is "pro" gay marriage/civil union laws. What types of appeals can you, the interviewer, use to gain information on this topic and present a compelling case for its legal status in all states?

◆ Report on the last time you were at the mall and were stopped by a sales associate to look at or try a new product.

◇ What did this individual say to you?

◇ How did you respond?

◇ What persuasion strategies were used?

◇ How did it end?

d i s c u s s i o n   q u e s t i o n s

◆ At the beginning of the year (January) you think it is a great idea to talk with your employer about having a HUGE Christmas in July sale. You think that you could increase sales exponentially during the summer months when your store is kind of slow. How could you persuade your employer to do this? What might you include in your Persuasive Interview to accomplish your goal?

◆ Discuss an instance where you were the interviewee/persuadee in a Persuasive Interview and reflect upon this instance and the information in your textbook. How could you have been a more informed participant during that interaction?

◆ How important are ethos, logos, and pathos during the Persuasive Interview?

◆ How important is language choice to the success of a Persuasive Interview?

◆ How can persuaders prevent polarizing their potential persuadees?

◆ Have you ever worked in a sales position? If so describe your strengths in this job. What were some difficulties that you faced?

◆ Are emotions used in Persuasive Interviews? How important are they?

◆ Is persuasion also considered manipulation?

◆ How can you win trust during a Persuasive Interview?

Ethics and Persuasion

You just got a job on campus (it is your junior year). You were hired by the Admissions Office on your campus and will begin giving prospective students and parents information about your institution of higher learning. While at the University you've been involved on campus in several organizations where you've held leadership positions and you've had experience in residence hall life as a resident assistant. Now, as an employee of the Admissions Office one of your primary tasks is to give campus tours. In this role you will not only be a guide through campus, but will become a representative of your institution and provide many valuable pieces of information. In some cases, you could be persuading these students and parents to enroll at your university

Consider the following:

♦ What do you think the Director of the Admissions Office would tell you your primary duties of this job should be? What do you think it should be? Please write out your answers to these questions.

♦ On each tour, what do you think the Director of Admissions would say your primary goal should be? What do you think it should be?

♦ Every campus wants to look its best to prospective students and parents but often times these campus visitors ask difficult questions. How would you respond to the following situation which might occur during one of your tours:

  ◊ *Hypothetical Instance:* A parent asks, "Our daughter, Paige, really wants to attend this university but as you know, we live 750 miles away. We are concerned for her safety. We wonder about how frequently parties occur, what kind of crime rates the city has, and what do you, as a student of this university, think of campus safety? How about residence hall safety?"

Note: You live in the halls and have seen, from time to time, other resident assistants not write up some students for alcohol and other drug violations. Additionally, you know that there have been a few fights on campus and many instances of petty theft over the last year and a half, yet campus police have not found the culprits.

   Write out the best response you could give. Do you consider it to be persuasive? Is your response fair to the inquiring parent? Your institution? To Paige? To yourself?

♦ After you've spent the afternoon with Paige and her parents, your campus tour is now coming to a close. How do you close this interaction? Are there things that you could say to persuade or encourage Paige to attend your institution?

Name _____ Date _____

Persuasive Interview

Please read the following scenario and then answer the questions.

The interviewer is a sales associate from Shiny New Car Dealership. This dealership is highly reputable in town and has been in business for over 50 years. Greg, the interviewer, met Jennifer at a tent show that the dealership was having at the mall a few weeks ago. At the time, she seemed very interested in the new car that she looked at (moon roof, fully loaded), but hasn't been back to the lot yet. Sales on the lot have been really slow and loan rates are low for new buyers.

Jennifer is a young mother of two who is an employed social worker. Her yearly income is $35,000. Currently, Jennifer is driving a 1990 minivan that has over 100,000 miles but still runs great. She has thought often about buying a new car, especially since she has two young children and because loan rates are so low. However, she isn't sure that she should buy a new car because hers has not given her any trouble. "Why throw out the old when the old still works," Jennifer would say.

Jennifer sees Greg as friendly but is leery of car salesmen because she thinks they are just out to make a quick dollar.

1. What are the most important personal characteristics/attitudes of Jennifer?

2. What are the major advantages of the persuasive situation?

3. What are the major disadvantages of the persuasive situation?

Persuasive Selling

Recall a time when you were persuaded to make a major purchase (automobile, computer, jewelry, musical instrument, etc.). Answer the following questions regarding this purchase:

1. Did the interviewer win your trust? Is so, how?

2. How did the interviewer adapt and tailor the agenda to you?

3. How did the interviewer open and close the interview?

4. How did the interviewer encourage you to elaborate and share information?

5. How did you prepare prior to making this purchase?

Recall a time when you were NOT persuaded to make a major purchase (automobile, computer, jewelry, musical instrument, etc.). Answer the following question regarding this purchase:

1. What could the interviewer have done differently in order to persuade you to make this purchase? Be specific and integrate material from your text in your response.

Persuasion Scenarios

Choose one of the following scenarios and explain how you would prepare and structure your Persuasive Interview. Make sure to incorporate information from your text in your response (i.e., what research is needed, what strategies, motives, values, and questions you would incorporate into your Persuasive Interview, and how you would open and close your interview). Write your response in essay format.

1. You want to persuade your employer to have a holiday party during the early part of December for the employees rather than the traditional Christmas party which is held one week prior to Christmas.

2. You want to persuade your supervisor to give you two extra days of vacation so you can attend your best friend's wedding in Mexico.

3. You want to persuade your supervisor in the cosmetic department of an upscale department store to offer a "buy one, get one free" sale for the most expensive beauty products in the store.

4. You want to persuade a young couple to purchase a minivan from you.

5. You are a survey taker and want to persuade the next customer at the local mall (where you are conducting your surveys) to complete your survey on shopping preferences.

6. You are one of eight applicants interviewing for the entry level sales manager position at XWF Company. You want to persuade the interviewer that you are the best applicant for the position.

7. You want to persuade the head of human resources at your company to hire two part-time employees to help with the work load.

8. You are the recruiting officer for the local student organization you belong to and are trying to persuade your friends to join this organization.

REFERENCES

Adler, R., & Elmhorst, J. M. (2010). *Communicating at work: Principles and practices for business and the professions.* (10th ed.). New York, NY: McGraw Hill.

Anderson, R., & Killenberg, G. (2009). *Interviewing: Speaking, listening and learning for professional life.* (2nd ed.). New York, NY: Oxford University Press.

Anderson, R. & Killenberg, G. (2009). *Instructor's resource guide for interviewing: Speaking, listening and learning for professional life.* New York, NY: Oxford University Press.

Barone, J., & Switzer, J. (1995). *Interviewing: Art and skill.* Boston, MA: Allyn & Bacon.

Blodgett, P. (1997). Six ways to be a better listener. *Training & Development*, July, 11–12.

Brownell, J. (2010). *Listening: Attitudes, principles and skills.* Boston, MA: Allyn & Bacon.

Darling, D. (2003). *The networking survival guide: Get the success you want by tapping into the people you know.* New York, NY: McGraw Hill.

Davis, M., Paleg, K. & Fanning, P. (2004). *The messages workbook: Powerful strategies for effective communication at work & home.* Oakland, CA: New Harbinger.

Evans, D., Hearn, M., Uhlemann, M., & Ivey, A. (2011). *Essential interviewing: A programmed approach to effective communication.* (8th ed.). Belmont, CA: Cengage.

Frank, M. (1986). *How to get your point across in 30 seconds or less.* New York, NY: Simon and Schuster.

Foster-Kuehn, M. & Wood, J. *Instructor resource manual for communication mosaics: An introduction to the field of communication.* (6th ed.). Belmont, CA: Thomson Wadsworth.

Gottlieb, M. (1986). *Interview.* White Plains, NY: Longman.

Moltz, D. (2009, October 23). Are today's grads unprofessional [Inside Higher Ed]? Retrieved from http://www.wiu.edu.insidehighered.com/news/2009/1023/professionalism.

Newman, L. (2007). *Careers in communication.* Dubuque, IA: Kendall/Hunt.

Nycz, M. (2010). Developing your 60 second commercial. *2010 AAEE Job Search Handbook*, 43.

Overston-Healy, J. (2008). The telephone interview: Your new job is calling. *2008 AAEE Job Search Handbook*, 25.

Petress, K. (1999). Listening: A vital skill. *Journal of Instructional Psychology, 26*(4), 261–262.

Powell, L. & Amsbary, J. (2006). *Interviewing: Situations and contexts.* Boston, MA: Allyn & Bacon.

Quintanilla, K., & Wahl, S. (2011). *Business and professional communication: Keys for workplace excellence.* Thousand Oaks, CA: Sage.

Salopek, J. (1999). Is anyone listening? *Training & Development*, September, 58–59.

Shelton, J. (2008). There's a new game in town: Successful interviewing in the electronic age. *2008 AAEE Job Search Handbook*, 24–25.

Stewart, C. (2008). *Interviewing principles and practices: Applications and exercises.* Dubuque, IA: Kendall/Hunt.

Stewart, C., & Cash, W. (2008). *Interviewing: Principles and practices.* (12th ed.). New York, NY: McGraw Hill.

Stewart, C., & Cash, W. (2011). *Interviewing: Principles and practices.* (13th ed.). New York, NY: McGraw Hill.

Ward, J.R. (1990). Now hear this: Without listening there is no communication. *Communication World, 7,* (7), 20.

Wood, J. (2011). *Communication mosaics: An introduction to the field of communication.* (6th ed.). Belmont, CA: Thomson Wadsworth.